ENVIRONMENT ACTION PLAN 2024–2030

TOWARD A NATURE-POSITIVE ASIA AND THE PACIFIC

NOVEMBER 2024

ASIAN DEVELOPMENT BANK

CONTENTS

FIGURES AND BOXES

Figures

Boxes

ACKNOWLEDGMENTS

The preparation of this Environment Action Plan 2024–2030 (EAP) was led by Karma Yangzom together with the entire Asian Development Bank (ADB) Environment group and guidance from Yoko Watanabe. The core team of the Environment Action Plan included Katrina Jayme and Umang Bhattarai, as well as Suzanne Robertson and Darline Lim at the early stage. The team is grateful for the support and guidance of the Climate Change and Sustainable Development senior management team that included Bruno Carrasco and Toru Kubo.

This EAP could not have been prepared without the ownership and commitment of many staff members from departments across ADB, namely members of the EAP working group: Aiming Zhou, Alexandra Galperin, Andrew Clinton, Ashok Srivastava, Au Shion Yee, Bimbika Sijapati Basnett, Brian Riley, Chris Dickinson, Collette You-Jung Shin, Declan Magee, F. Cleo Kawawaki, Fei Yu, Francesco Ricciardi, Henry Young Choi, Jacob Sorensen, Jeffrey Taylor, Jennifer Romero-Torres, Ji Seon Kim, Kristina Katich, Lin Lu, Luis Antonio L. Lagdameo III, Mark Kunzer, Martino Pelli, Mian S. Shafi, Michelle Ann E. Ramirez, Miko Jazmine J. Mojica, Paolo Manunta, Rogerio De Almeida Vieira De Sa, Roka Sanda, Rustam Ishenaliev, Saad Abdullah Paracha, Setijo Boentaran, Shobhna Decloitre, Sibesh Bhattacharya, Siddhartha Shah, Umang Bhattarai, Wilhelmina T. Paz, Yasmin Siddiqi, and many other colleagues, especially those who supported the working group members.

Resident missions, nongovernmental organization center, and the office of safeguards provided invaluable support in organizing consultations and dialogues with representatives from the governments, civil society organizations, and Indigenous Peoples.

The Environment group thanks the ADB Board of Directors for their guidance and strong engagement, and Vice President Fatima Yasmin, Woochong Um, and Warren Evans for their strategic vision and guidance throughout the process. We are particularly grateful for the engagement and valuable inputs and feedback provided by the representatives from governments, civil society organizations and Indigenous Peoples.

Strong coordination and administrative support were provided by Agnes Patricia Magat, Allan Marcelino, Maria Charina Aguado, Maria Katrina Darauay, April dela Cruz, Karen Elec Lapitan, Marianne Villanueva, Pamela Elmido, and Zipporah Marquez.

David McCauley conducted initial research, consultations, and prepared the approach paper for the EAP; Jess Alfonso Macasaet edited the manuscript; and Rocilyn Locsin Laccay implemented typesetting, graphics, and layout. The Department of Communications and Knowledge Management facilitated the publication.

ABBREVIATIONS

ADB	Asian Development Bank
CAREC	Central Asia Regional Economic Cooperation Program
CCAP	Climate Change Action Plan
CCSD	Climate Change and Sustainable Development Department
CoP	Environment Community of Practice
CPS	country partnership strategy
CSO	civil society organization
DMC	developing member country
DRMAP	Disaster Risk Management Action Plan
EAP	Environment Action Plan
GDP	gross domestic product
GMS	Greater Mekong Subregion
MDB	multilateral development bank
MTR	Mid Term Review
OMDP	Office of Markets Development and Public-Private Partnership
PPFD	Procurement, Portfolio and Financial Management Department
PPP	public–private partnership
PSOD	Private Sector Operations Department
SASEC	South Asia Subregional Economic Cooperation
SDG	Sustainable Development Goals
SPD	Strategy, Policy, and Partnerships Department
TA	technical assistance

EXECUTIVE SUMMARY

The Environment Action Plan 2024–2030 (EAP) guides the strategic response of the Asian Development Bank (ADB) to the triple planetary crisis of biodiversity loss, pollution, and climate change. It sets out ADB's commitment in responding to this crisis and expanding the scope and scale of related investments in collaboration with key partners.

The EAP comprises three closely linked and mutually supportive strategic pillars as solutions to the crisis: (i) biodiversity and ecosystem management, (ii) pollution control and circular economy, and (iii) nature-based climate solutions. The EAP thus is in full alignment with ADB operations that contribute to clusters of interconnected Sustainable Development Goals related to people, planet, and prosperity. It outlines the operational road map for ADB's expanded role in supporting its developing member countries (DMCs) in addressing the region and country's key environmental challenges by conserving environment and nature as a vehicle for economic growth and improved livelihoods.

The EAP proposes two distinct but complementary approaches: increasing nature-positive investments and mainstreaming environment into sector operations and investments. This entails redefining priorities and refining environmental diagnostics across DMCs and regions, generating and sharing knowledge on priority and emerging environment and nature related issues. It ensures the strategic integration of environmental priorities into country partnership strategies at the upstream level; identifying policy and regulatory measures to create an enabling environment, integrating environment priorities into ADB programming exercises, and developing a pipeline of programs and projects at the midstream level; and implementing needed assessments and studies, and developing and implementing both public and private sector investments at the downstream level. The EAP has also identified four cross-cutting measures across the three streams. These measures will enhance cross-sectoral integration, approaches to conserve regional public goods, and enhance natural capital. It identifies 13 action areas that are time-bound with clear interdepartmental responsibility and accountability (Appendix 1).

The EAP recognizes that the peoples and economies throughout the world depend heavily on a healthy environment and nature. Approximately half of Asia and the Pacific's economy is directly dependent on products and services provided by nature and biodiversity, and associated ecosystems. Protection and restoration of healthy ecosystems is key to solving climate mitigation and adaptation and the planetary emergencies. The increasing environmental degradation in the region not only hampers economic progress, but also threatens public health and well-being, particularly vulnerable populations including women and girls, Indigenous Peoples and local communities, and people with disabilities. The EAP calls for integrated solutions to address the interconnected challenges of climate change, biodiversity loss, and pollution, including the need for valuing ecosystem services in markets and national accounting.

The EAP builds on the Environmental Operational Directions from 2013 to 2020 and is fully consistent with ADB's Strategy 2030. It is aligned with its midterm review and the five strategic focus areas of climate action, private sector development, regional cooperation and public goods, digital transformation and resilience and empowerment. The EAP was developed through a consultative process involving ADB's Board, Management, Staff, and external stakeholders, including civil society organizations and Indigenous Peoples, and other partners. The EAP promotes the One ADB approach and contributes to the four operational shifts under the New Operating Model (NOM) of climate change, private sector, solutions-orientation, and new ways of working.

The EAP aligns ADB's operations with key multilateral environmental agreements and strategies, including the Kunming–Montreal Global Biodiversity Framework, Paris Agreement, and the upcoming Global Plastic Treaty. It also operationalizes ADB's commitment under the Joint Statement by the Multilateral Development Banks on Nature, People, and Planet.

ADB aims to address the triple planetary crisis and promote sustainable development by making the environment a core focus of its climate change and private sector shifts. Environment, climate change mitigation and adaptation, and disaster risk management are closely interconnected. The EAP will work in synergy with the ADB's Climate Change Action Plan and Disaster Risk Management Action Plan through integrated planning and implementation, complementary financing and investments, coordinated capacity development initiatives, knowledge management and communication efforts, and synergies in monitoring and reporting frameworks.

EAP will work across all sectors such as agriculture, transport, health, energy, finance and urban development to enhance nature positive investments and mainstream environment sustainability in sector operations. Furthermore, ADB will incorporate gender responsive approaches and address the specific needs of fragile and conflict-affected situations and small island developing states, and promote community-based approaches in nature-based solutions. ADB's approach aims at safeguarding vulnerable populations including Indigenous Peoples and local communities from environmental harm while empowering them to participate in decision-making and operation processes.

All departments across ADB will work toward the successful implementation of the EAP. Responsibilities are allocated along business processes to integrate environmental sustainability into various operational tasks. The Climate Change and Sustainable Development Department will provide thought leadership and be responsible for the overall coordination, facilitation, and tracking of the EAP implementation. Sector groups will play a critical role in leading the processing and implementation of nature-positive investment and mainstreaming environment in sector operations. Regional departments and resident missions will promote nature-positive investments and mainstreaming environment in sector operations complementing and building on safeguards compliance. The Private Sector Operations Department and the Office of Markets Development and Public–Private Partnership will engage with the private sector and provide advisory services to DMCs. Non-operational corporate departments will play a major role in reducing institutional barriers and creating an enabling corporate environment for mainstreaming environmental sustainability into ADB operations.

The list of environment actions will be reviewed and updated annually, with a midterm review of the EAP in 2027 and a final report in 2030 to assess results and draw lessons for future strategies. A robust monitoring and results framework will be established, aligned with the corporate results framework, to track progress. Annual progress reports will be prepared and shared with the Board for information.

I RATIONALE

Introduction

The Environment Action Plan 2024–2030 (EAP) guides the strategic response of the Asian Development Bank (ADB) to the triple planetary crisis facing humanity, namely biodiversity loss, pollution, and climate change. It sets ADB's commitment in responding to this crisis and expanding the scope and scale of related investments in collaboration with key partners. The EAP comprises three closely linked and mutually supportive strategic pillars as solutions to the crisis (Figure 1): (i) biodiversity and ecosystem management, (ii) pollution control and circular economy, and (iii) nature-based climate solutions. The EAP thus is in full alignment with ADB operations that contribute to clusters of interconnected Sustainable Development Goals (SDGs) related to people, planet, and prosperity. It outlines the operational road map for ADB's expanded role in supporting its developing member countries (DMCs) in addressing the region and country's key environmental challenges and by conserving environment and nature as a vehicle for economic growth and improved livelihoods.

Two distinct but complementary approaches are proposed: (i) increase nature-positive investments; and (ii) mainstream environmental sustainability into sector operations and investments, while tailor-fitting operational support to the specific context of DMCs. This entails redefining priorities and refining environmental diagnostics across DMCs and regions, knowledge generation and sharing on priority and emerging environment and nature related issues. It ensures the strategic integration of environmental priorities into country partnership strategies at the upstream level; identifying policy and regulatory measures to create an enabling environment, integrating environment priorities into ADB programming exercises, and developing a pipeline of projects at the midstream level; and conducting needed assessments and studies, and developing and implementing both public and private sector investments at the downstream level. The EAP has also identified four cross-cutting measures across the three streams. These measures will enhance cross-sectoral integration, approaches to conserving regional public goods, and enhance natural capital. It identifies 13 action areas that are time-bound with clear interdepartmental responsibility and accountability (Appendix 1).

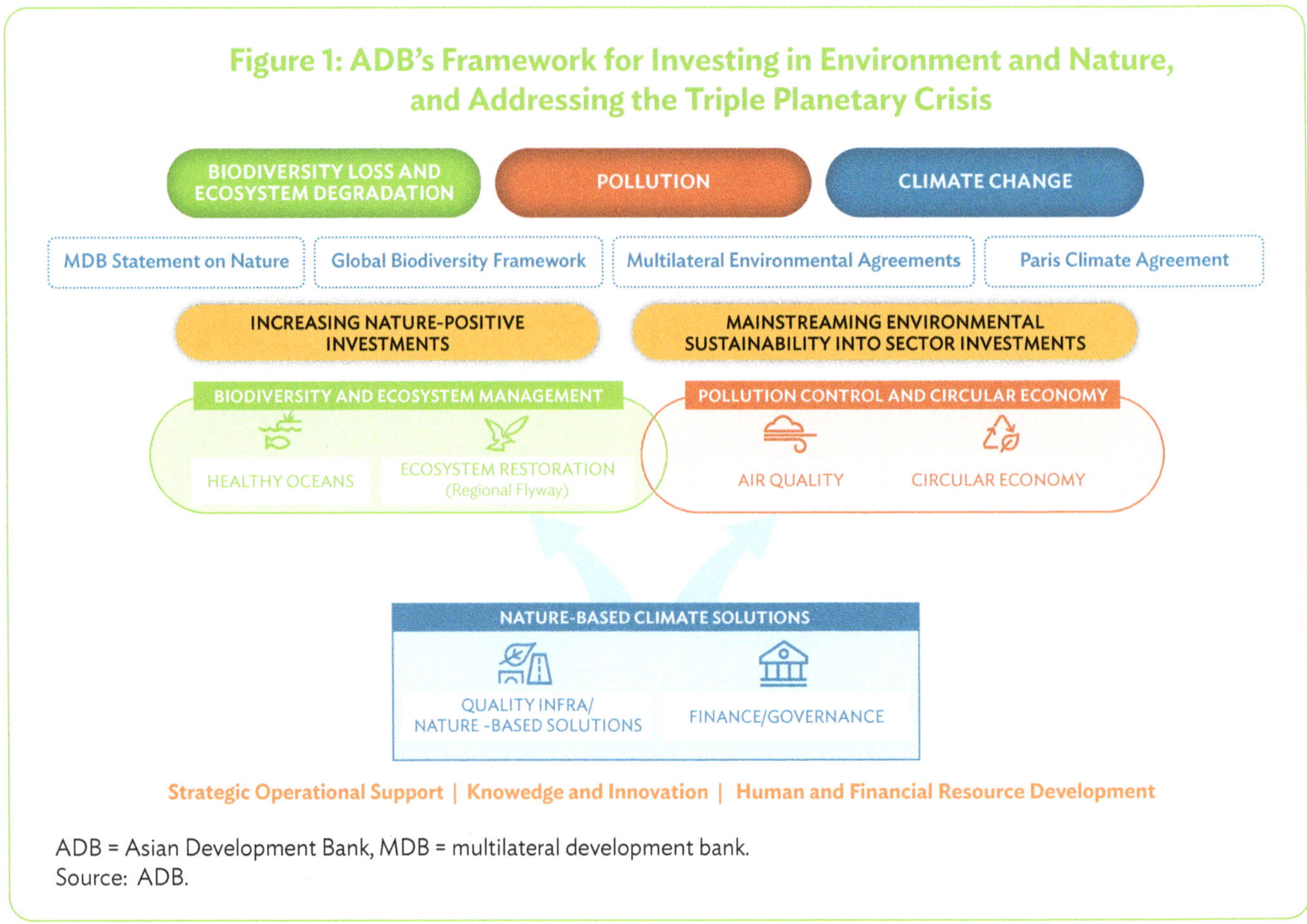

ADB = Asian Development Bank, MDB = multilateral development bank.
Source: ADB.

The EAP is fully consistent with ADB's Strategy 2030 and the five focus areas identified in its Midterm Review (MTR): (i) climate action, (ii) private sector development, (iii) regional cooperation and public goods (Box 1), (iv) digital transformation, and (v) resilience and empowerment. The EAP will complement implementation of environmental safeguards requirements under the forthcoming Environmental and Social Framework of ADB. It is also fully aligned with the four shifts under ADB's new operating model: climate change, private sector development, solutions, and new ways of working (section II). Given the strong complementarities between environment, climate change, and disaster risk management as a cluster, the EAP serves as part of a series of action plans that includes the Climate Change Action Plan (CCAP) approved in November 2023, and the Disaster Risk Management Action Plan (DRMAP) approved in October 2024.

The EAP is developed through a consultative process with the Board, Management, and Staff, as well as external stakeholders and partners and serves as a guidance document for ADB staff. The action list in Appendix 1 will be a living document and subject to review and updates on an annual basis. The main text will undergo a midterm review in 2027 and be updated to ensure ADB's continued effectiveness and responsiveness to dynamic global developments and changing circumstances among its DMCs. Under the One ADB approach, with the leadership and facilitating roles of Climate Change and Sustainable Development Department (CCSD) through its Environment group, all departments across ADB are responsible and will work together for the successful implementation of the EAP, enabling ADB's leadership in environment and nature investment and supporting ADB's position as the climate bank of Asia and the Pacific.

Box 1: Environment and Nature as Regional Public Goods

Enhancing regional cooperation and public goods is one of the five strategic focus areas identified under the Strategy 2030 Midterm Review. Examples of regional public goods supported by the Asian Development Bank (ADB) include regional health security, macroeconomic policy coordination and prevention of financial contagion, transboundary management of environmental services, and climate change mitigation and adaptation. Ecosystems and their natural resources could cut across national boundaries and their conservation and sustainable use require collective efforts. ADB's long-term work in protecting the Mekong River Basin is a prime example of a regional public good because of its inherent regional use as a shared resource. The Mekong River is shared by six countries and use of the river affects flood control, water availability for agriculture, water quality, fisheries, hydropower, navigation, and ecosystem conservation. Multilateral development banks like ADB can help to narrow knowledge and financing gaps, provide platforms for continuous dialogue, and serve as honest brokers to enhance mutual trust between countries. Moreover, coordination among global, regional, and subregional institutions can enhance complementarity and alignment of goals and strategies.

Source: ADB Strategy 2030 Midterm Review.

Current Context and Issues

The peoples and economies throughout the world depend heavily on a healthy environment and nature. About half of global gross domestic product (GDP)—approximately $44 trillion—is either directly or indirectly dependent on products and services provided by nature and biodiversity, and associated ecosystems.[1] In Asia and the Pacific, about $18 trillion or over 53% of the region's economy is recognized as directly dependent on nature. Among these, the sectors with higher direct dependence on nature include construction, agriculture and food systems, fishery and aquaculture, and forestry, accounting for around $7 trillion in Asia.[2]

Asia and the Pacific countries accounted for over 70% of global GDP growth over the past decade, and GDP per capita is growing much faster in Asia than in any other region.[3] However, the impressive economic advancements made in the region over the past decades unfortunately have come, in part, through significant environmental costs, including severe ecosystem degradation and pollution. The UN Economic and Social Commission for Asia and the Pacific notes that Asia has undergone the most rapid and serious decline in biodiversity and ecosystem services.[4] It states that during the past 3 decades, forest areas in Southeast Asia declined by 48.7 million hectares. This decrease has been primarily driven by an increase in timber extraction and the conversion of land for agriculture and aquaculture. During the same period, mangrove areas—which provide a wide range of benefits in terms of carbon sequestration, coastal protection, natural products, and tourism—declined by 403,000 hectares (footnote 4). Air and water pollution, along with solid waste management, also continue to be a challenge in the region, particularly in highly urbanized areas. The region's exposure to air pollution increased by 10% above the global average during the same period (footnote 4). Despite efforts to reduce air pollution in various subregions,

---

[1]   World Economic Forum. 2020. *Nature Risk Rising: Why the Crisis Engulfing Nature Matters for Business and the Economy*.

[2]   Asia Investor Group on Climate Change and PwC. 2024. New research: Over half of Asia Pacific's economy directly dependent on nature. 24 April.

[3]   World Economics. Asia and Pacific.

[4]   United Nations Economic and Social Commission for Asia and the Pacific. 2022. *Protecting our planet through regional cooperation and solidarity in Asia and the Pacific*.

particularly in Southeast Asia, East Asia, and the Pacific, most cities in the region continue to experience high levels of ambient air pollution, which is often linked to health risks and morbidity. It is recognized that 99 out of the 100 cities with the most polluted air are located in Asia.[5] Additionally, although the Asia and Pacific region is one of the largest producers of wastewater, it has one the lowest rates of collection and treatment.[6] Moreover, according to research, 80% of all plastic waste found in the ocean comes from rivers in Asia.[7]

Biodiversity loss can have serious economic consequences for economies, livelihoods, and well-being.[8] The World Economic Forum reported that 63% of the GDP in Asia and the Pacific ($19.5 trillion) risks losses from nature depletion, positioning the region "at the heart of the global biodiversity crisis."[9] Asia and the Pacific is recognized with its exceptional biodiversity value by housing more than half of the megadiverse countries globally.[10] The region's rich natural resources are vital for its economy and sustainable livelihoods. Ensuring access to ecosystem services like food, materials, and clean air and water is crucial for improved livelihood and poverty alleviation as well as overall cultural, spiritual, and economic well-being of populations.[11] Conversely, a transition to nature-positive development could generate an annual $10 trillion in business opportunities globally by 2030 while creating 395 million jobs each year. Asia and the Pacific could contribute more than $4 trillion to this business value and account for 232 million of these jobs (footnote 11).

The reasons for environmental deterioration in the region are multifaceted, including urbanization, intensification of agriculture, rising energy use and transportation, changing production patterns and consumer behavior, and population growth and poverty. These have led to land conversion and degradation for agriculture and industry, urban sprawl and infrastructure expansion, over exploitation of natural resources, resource inefficiency and waste generation, and unsustainable supply chain practices in industries. These unsound socioeconomic activities—in absence of adequate policies and regulations and their enforcement, and limited capacity for implementing and monitoring solutions, such as pollution and depletion or erosion of natural capital—exert pressures on the region's environment that degrade air, land, soils, freshwater, and marine ecosystems, consequently limiting the prosperity of people that support livelihood, industry, and economy.

In 2020, the United Nations system used the term *triple planetary crisis* to inform the three key interlinked environmental, social, economic and health challenges that humanity currently faces: climate change, pollution, and biodiversity loss.[12] Each of these issues have their own causes and effects but they converge and reinforce each other.[13] Climate change is an urgent global challenge with long-term shifts in temperatures and weather patterns that inevitably will completely alter ecosystems that support life on the planet. Environmental pollution, including air pollution, is the largest cause of disease and premature deaths in the world. Finally, biodiversity loss leads to decline in natural capital, ecosystem services, and reduced resilience to disasters, which has detrimental impacts to all facets of human life.[14]

---

[5]   IQAir. 2024. 2023 IQAir World Air Quality Report.

[6]   E. R. Jones et sl. 2021. Country-level and gridded estimates of wastewater production, collection, treatment and reuse. *Earth Systems Science Data.* 13 (2).

[7]   L. Meijer et al. 2021. More than 1,000 rivers account for 80% of global riverine plastic emissions into the ocean. *Science Advances.* 7(18).

[8]   P. Dasgupta. 2021. *The Economics of Biodiversity: The Dasgupta Review,* Final Report of the Independent Review on the Economics of Biodiversity.

[9]   Temasek, World Economic Forum, and Alphabeta. 2021. New Nature Economy: Asia's Next Wave. September.

[10]   United Nations Economic and Social Commission for Asia and the Pacific. 2019. Investing in biodiversity and ecosystems. April.

[11]   Intergovernmental Science-Policy Platform on Biodiversity and Ecosystem Services. 2018. Regional Assessment Report on Biodiversity and Ecosystem Services for Asia and the Pacific. Bonn, Germany.

[12]   UNEP. 2020. The triple planetary crisis: Forging a new relationship between people and the earth. 14 July.

[13]   L. Estrada. 2024. The triple planetary crisis: What is it and what can we do about it? *AIDA.* 30 January.

[14]   United Nations Framework Convention on Climate Change. 2022. What is the Triple Planetary Crisis? 13 April.

Climate change itself has become a significant driver of biodiversity loss and ecosystem degradation, including species reduction and extinctions, influencing shifts in the distribution of ecosystems, plants, and animals, and leading to increased infectious diseases. Responding to these global concerns can and must be done in an integrated manner by linking attention and action between climate and nature.

Maintaining and restoring healthy ecosystems plays a key role in dealing with the causes and consequences of climate change. Historically, deforestation accounts for 30% of carbon emissions globally. Today, forest loss and damage are the cause of around 10% of global warming. Agriculture is also recognized as a major contributor to climate change. Overall, agriculture, forestry, and other land use represents around one-fifth (22%) of human-caused greenhouse gas emissions.[15]

Healthy ecosystems, particularly forests and oceans, provide valuable services to the economy and society in addressing climate change. Forests continuously remove carbon from the atmosphere acting as a long-term reservoir while supporting very high biodiversity, helping purify water and air, and providing sustainable livelihoods for millions. Wetlands and coastal mangroves play similarly significant roles in removing atmospheric carbon and storing it in vegetation and soils. Oceans generate 50% of oxygen on earth, absorb 25% of fossil fuel-based carbon dioxide emissions, and capture 90%[16] of the excess heat generated by these emissions. Further, land plants and trees can net sequester an additional 25% of emissions along with contributions from coastal ecosystems, agricultural soils, and wetlands. [17]

Moreover, healthy ecosystems offer enormous and cost-effective climate adaptation benefits. Coastal ecosystems can be particularly effective at maintaining or building climate resilience by protecting against erosion and reducing flood risks from storm surges and high winds. Likewise, forested watersheds serve as a buffer to manage natural water cycle alterations when an area faces either too little or too much precipitation, including from extreme rainfall events, and help soil retention through prevention of sediment runoff. However, since these benefits are often not recognized with a monetary value, ecosystems and natural capital are largely not considered in policy and decision-making, resulting in mismanagement and overexploitation. The cost of the degradation of ecosystems could reach $9.87 trillion globally between 2011 and 2050. Notably, 4[18] out of the 10 countries most affected by these losses are situated in Asia and the Pacific.[19] Furthermore, the proactive preservation and restoration of these natural systems are also crucial to prevent tipping points—critical points of no return that could disrupt the global climate system and the biodiversity it supports. For example, the loss of coral reefs and rainforests, both of which are nearing their ecological thresholds, would result in the extinction of thousands of species and the loss of ecosystem services that millions of people rely on for food, water, and economic needs.

Whether to achieve climate mitigation, adaptation or both, the protection and restoration of healthy ecosystems is key to solving these planetary emergencies and their manifestations in the region that not only hamper economic progress, but also threaten public health and well-being, particularly vulnerable populations including women and girls, Indigenous Peoples and local communities, and people with disabilities. Adverse effects to public health outcomes include increased incidence of respiratory diseases due to air pollution, waterborne diseases from contaminated water sources, and mental health issues linked to the loss of green spaces. Addressing these environmental challenges can lead to substantial improvements in public health (Box 2).

---

[15]   US Environmental Protection Agency. Global Greenhouse Gas Overview.

[16]   United Nations Regional Information Centre for Western Europe. 2023. Global warming: 90% of emissions heat absorbed by the oceans. 25 September.

[17]   NOAA National Environmental Satellite, Data and Information Service. Ocean-Atmosphere CO_2 Exchange.

[18]   New Zealand, Singapore, Sri Lanka, and Viet Nam.

[19]   2020. WWF-UK. Roxburgh, T., Ellis, K., Johnson, J.A., Baldos, U.L., Hertel, T., Nootenboom, C., and Polasky, S. 2020. Global Futures: Assessing the global economic impacts of environmental change to support policymaking. Summary report, January 2020.

Box 2: Environment and Health Nexus

Biodiversity and ecosystem management. Healthy ecosystems provide numerous health benefits, such as reducing urban heat island effects, improving mental health through access to green spaces, and preventing vector-borne diseases by maintaining balanced ecosystems.

Pollution management and circular economy. Air and water pollution pose serious risks to both current and future generations, such as reduced life expectancy, cognitive impairment in children, and increased incidence of respiratory diseases such as asthma and chronic obstructive pulmonary disease. Effective pollution management strategies, focusing on both outdoor and indoor air pollution, are essential for improving public health. Ensuring clean water and proper sanitation is crucial for preventing water-borne diseases. Projects should include measures for continuous monitoring and improvement of water sources used for drinking and sanitation. Integrating these measures within a circular economy framework, which emphasizes resource reuse and pollution reduction, will promote improved long-term health and well-being, particularly for vulnerable people including women, youth, and others who are disproportionately impacted.

Nature-based climate solutions. Implementation of nature-based solutions enhances community resilience and adaptation capacities, which are critical for public health. For example, mangrove restoration projects protect against storm surges and support local fisheries, improving food security and nutrition. Access to natural spaces has been shown to reduce stress and improve psychological well-being.

Finally, the importance of nature is not limited to its direct economic contributions and climate change benefit. Nature holds tremendous historical and cultural value in Asia and the Pacific and is the source of traditional knowledge, including on land and natural resources management. Many Asian and Pacific cultures recognize nature as integral to their spiritual and philosophical beliefs, revering both the living and nonliving elements of ecosystems while recognizing that humans are part of the living world. Indigenous Peoples and local communities across the region often have particularly strong cultural and spiritual ties to nature, and many have developed rich knowledge systems based on their longstanding interactions with ecosystems. Indigenous Peoples are recognized as stewards of the environment, protecting over 80% of the remaining biodiversity. [20] Meanwhile, environmental challenges such as deforestation, air pollution, and climate change have had an outsized impact on Indigenous Peoples, ethnic minorities, and marginalized groups across the Asia and Pacific region. Actions to address this crisis can inadvertently have negative consequences if the rights and knowledge of these peoples are not recognized, benefits and burdens are not equitably shared, and adequate representation is not ensured in decision making processes.[21]

---

[20] Government of Australia. 2021. State of the Environment.

[21] T.J. Forsyth. 2014. Climate justice is not just ice. *Geoforum*. 54. pp 230–232; R. Myers and M. Mohair. 2015. Searching for justice: Rights vs 'Benefits' in Bukit Baka Bukit Raya National Park, Indonesia. *Conservation and Society*. 13(4). pp. 370–381; T. Sikor and P. Newell. 2014. Globalizing Environmental Justice? *Geoforum*. 54. pp. 151–157.; and A. Martin et al. 2020. Environmental Justice and Transformations to Sustainability. *Environment: Science and Policy for Sustainable Development*. 62(6). pp. 19–30.

Opportunities and Challenges

The ongoing global environmental crisis refocuses attention and energies toward countries' commitments under more than 30 multilateral environment agreements, including (i) United Nations Climate Change Framework Convention; (ii) Convention on Biological Diversity; (iii) Convention to Combat Desertification; (iv) Basel, Rotterdam, and Stockholm Conventions; (v) Minamata Convention on Mercury; and (vi) Convention on Wetlands of International Importance especially as Water-fowl Habitat. Developing countries in Asia and the Pacific have ratified most of these global conventions and have committed to implementing the agreed decisions.

In December 2022, the Kunming–Montreal Global Biodiversity Framework was adopted at the 15th meeting of the Conference of the Parties to the Convention on Biological Diversity. The framework sets out an ambitious plan to implement broad-based action to bring about a transformation in our societies' relationship with biodiversity by 2030, including protection of at least 30% of lands, freshwaters, and oceans by 2030. This is in line with the 2030 Agenda for Sustainable Development and its SDGs and to ensure the shared vision of living in harmony with nature by 2050.

Multilateral development banks (MDBs), governments, private sector groups, and civil society organizations (CSOs) globally are intensifying efforts to protect and restore nature. In 2021, ADB signed the *Joint Statement by the Multilateral Development Banks: Nature, People and Planet.* The statement affirmed these banks' commitment to mainstreaming nature into their policies, analysis, assessments, advice, investments, and operations, pledging to work together to support a sustainable, inclusive, green, and resilient post-COVID-19 recovery. Moreover, environment-related global priorities are emerging from international political and economic fora like the G20 Principles for Quality Infrastructure Investment (2019), the Political leaders Pledge for Nature (2020), the G7 2030 Nature Compact (2021), and the G20 Bali Leaders Declaration (2022). As of this writing, the international community is preparing for a Global Plastics Treaty to combat plastic pollution.

At the same time, addressing environmental degradation poses numerous challenges apart from delivering systems solutions that match its complexity. One of the challenges is valuing the important economic functions of healthy ecosystems. The value of natural capital and the ecosystem services they provide are often not fully reflected in market pricing, thereby excluding them from national accounting, financial, and investment decisions and national financial reporting systems. Government and the private sector often lack the institutional knowledge, capacity, and awareness of ecosystem services, as the causes and impacts of ecosystem degradation are poorly documented and understood.

In addition, a major challenge in Asia and the Pacific is the limited governance capacity to manage regional public goods such as ecosystem services that provide benefits beyond national boundaries. Addressing climate and ecosystem challenges involves delivering global and regional public goods alongside generating local level benefits. These goods include non-excludable resources, services, and benefits, like oceans, the ozone layer, and ecosystems which offer benefits beyond countries' borders. Hence, there is a need to emphasize the importance of shared responsibilities across boundaries and strengthen governance systems.

With limited understanding of the value of nature, measures and investments to protect and restore the environment and nature are often not prioritized in domestic and international public and private financing in many countries. As such, there is limited focus on creating policies to guide business and finance sectors toward sustainable ecosystem and natural capital usage. Even though nature valuation tools are becoming increasingly available, governments and financial institutions have yet to play a strong role in promoting their use and incentivizing good practices or penalizing poor practices to enable environmental sustainability.

To address the substantial risks of nature and biodiversity loss (Box 3), it is recognized that ADB and other MDBs could take a key role in identifying and supporting implementation innovative mechanisms that can rapidly mobilize substantial financing for nature positive investments and reform harmful subsidies, such as those for agriculture.[22] For example, it is estimated that financial flows into global biodiversity conservation in 2019 were between $124 billion to $143 billion, while spending on agriculture, forestry, and fisheries subsidies that degrade nature was at least 2 to 4 times greater. Meanwhile, a financing gap of about $711 billion must be filled annually worldwide to reverse the decline of biodiversity.[23] Nature-positive investments and mainstreaming environmental sustainability in sector investments have the potential to yield multiple benefits, including substantial climate-related co-benefits, including carbon sequestration, adaptation, and resilience as well as direct health, employment, and livelihood benefits.

Box 3: Biodiversity and Nature

According to the officially adopted definition by the Convention on Biological Diversity, biodiversity is "the variability among living organisms from all sources including, inter alia, terrestrial, marine and other aquatic ecosystems and the ecological complexes of which they are part; this includes diversity within species, between species and of ecosystems." In other words, biodiversity is the part of nature that is alive and includes every living thing on Earth. On the other hand, nature is all the existing systems created at the same time as the Earth, all the features, forces and processes, such as the weather, the sea and mountains. In other words, nature is all life on Earth (i.e., biodiversity), together with the geology, water, climate and all other inanimate components that comprise our planet.

Source: Convention on Biological Diversity. Biodiversity and nature, close but not quite the same.

ADB's Practice and Experiences

ADB's vision is to achieve a prosperous, inclusive, resilient, and sustainable Asia and the Pacific, while sustaining its efforts to eradicate extreme poverty. The EAP will draw upon over 5 decades of environmental, social, and related expertise as it solidifies and expands its support to the DMCs in addressing biodiversity loss, pollution, and climate change. ADB's recent history supporting the environment shows a continuous evolution with three distinct phases (Figure 2). Under phase one, ADB supported environmental protection efforts across the region, applying strict environmental safeguards for its projects using the "do no harm" principle. This played a key role in reducing the negative environmental consequences of development investments supported by ADB. During the past decade, and under phase two, ADB expanded investments with the specific objective "to do good" in sector and thematic projects for positive environmental outcomes. These projects have supported DMCs to improve forest, water, coastal, marine or land management, including cleaning up key waterbodies and improving air quality and solid waste management. Now entering its third phase, ADB is tasked to raise its level of ambition to a new height, investing in environment and nature with significant scale up commitments. This EAP includes various recommendations on delivering environment operations at scale.

---

[22] Continuous spending on harmful subsidies for agriculture, forestry, and fisheries are key drivers of biodiversity loss. However, when designed to correct market failures or internalize positive externalities from ecosystems, subsidies can contribute to the protection of the environment and natural assets (e.g., tax concessions to energy developers for renewable energy development or e-vehicles).

[23] The Paulson Institute, The Nature Conservancy, and the Cornell Atkinson Center for Sustainability. Financing Nature: Closing the global biodiversity financing gap.

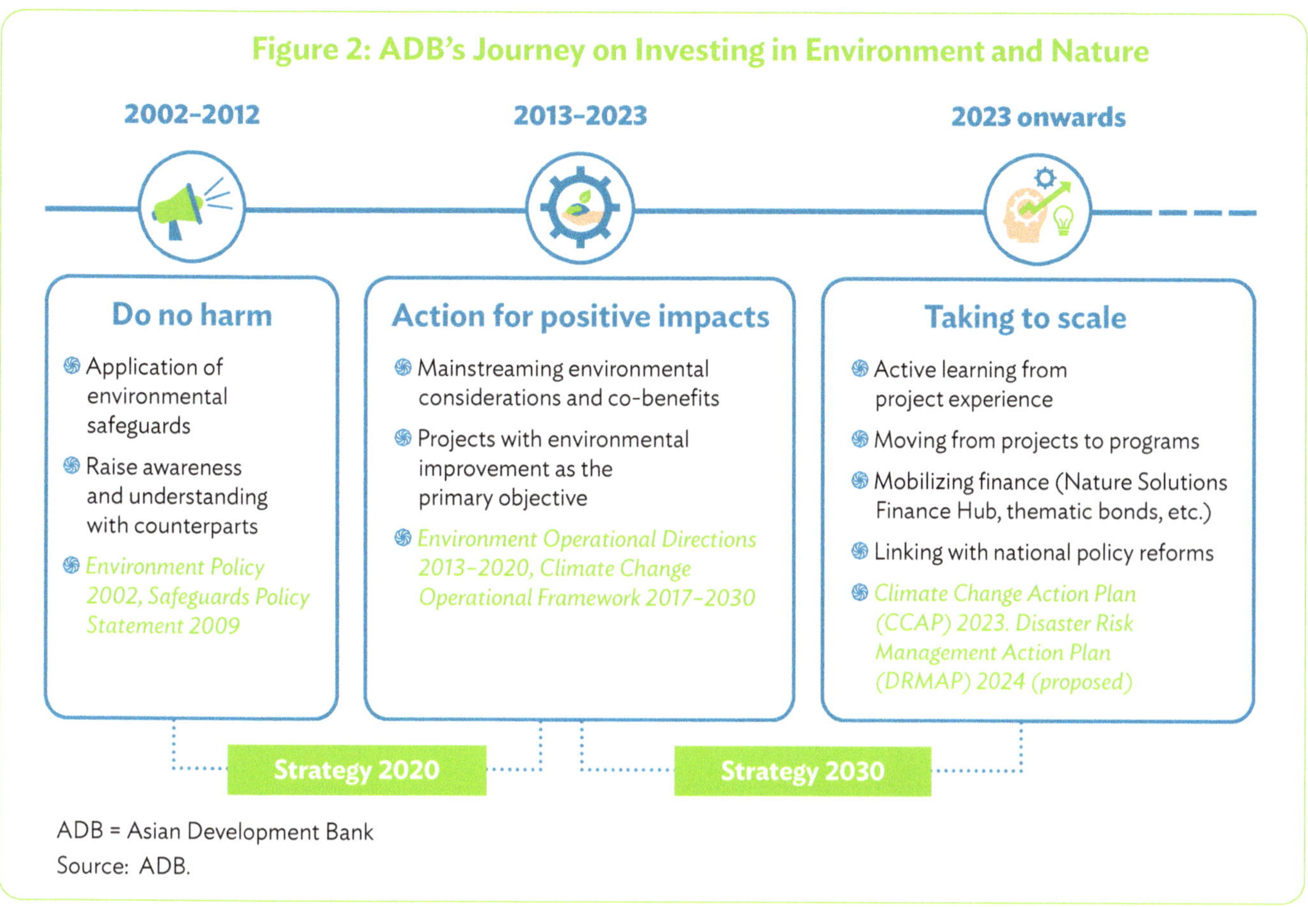

ADB = Asian Development Bank
Source: ADB.

Phase 1 (2002–2012): Safeguards and environmental sustainability. While ADB started working on environmental assessment for its investment projects as early as in 1979, at the turn of the millennium, ADB adopted an Environment Policy in 2002 that recognizes environmental sustainability (Box 4) to be a prerequisite for pro-poor economic growth and efforts to reduce poverty. By 2007, ADB issued its first Sustainability Report, providing information about the bank's continued work on promoting environmentally sustainable and inclusive growth, and on reducing its corporate footprint.[24] In 2008, ADB's long-term strategic framework, Strategy 2020 was in place, identifying environmentally sustainable growth as one of ADB's three main strategic agendas.[25] In 2009, ADB's Safeguard Policy Statement was developed to strengthen environment protection, better manage involuntary resettlement, and improve engagement with Indigenous Peoples. ADB's Safeguard Policy Statement affirmed that *environmental and social sustainability* were a cornerstone of economic growth and poverty reduction in Asia and the Pacific. It promoted the social and environmental sustainability of projects by (i) avoiding adverse impacts of projects on the environment and affected people, where possible; (ii) minimizing, mitigating, and/or compensating for adverse project impacts on the environment and affected people when avoidance is not possible; and (iii) helping borrowers and clients to strengthen their safeguard systems and develop the capacity to manage environmental and social risks.[26]

---

[24] ADB. ADB Sustainability Reports.

[25] ADB. 2008. *Strategy 2020: Working for an Asia and Pacific Free of Poverty*.

[26] ADB. 2009. Safeguard Policy Statement.

Box 4: Environmental Sustainability

Environmental Sustainability refers to a long-term development approach that ensures the conservation and management of natural resources, mitigates environmental degradation, and promotes eco-friendly practices, to (i) meet the needs of the present without compromising the ability of future generations to meet their own needs, and (ii) protect the shared environment—air, water, land, and ecosystems—in ways that are economically viable, beneficial to human health and well-being, and socially just in the long term.

Adapted from United States Environmental Protection Agency definition of sustainability.

Phase 2 (2013–2023): Environmentally sustainable growth and expanding environment-related projects.
In 2013, ADB's Environmental Operational Directions, 2013–2020 was developed to support the region's transition to environmentally sustainable growth through (i) a shift to sustainable infrastructure, (ii) investing in natural capital, (iii) strengthening environmental governance and management capacity, and (iv) addressing climate change.[27] With the growing portfolio and projects on climate change, disaster risk management, and environmental sustainability, by 2016, an Independent Evaluation Department strategic review reported that "ADB has laid a foundation that will enable it to become the environmental sustainability bank for the region."[28]

Finally, in 2018, ADB adopted Strategy 2030 and its vision of a prosperous, inclusive, resilient, and sustainable Asia and the Pacific. Tackling climate change, building climate and disaster resilience, and enhancing environmental sustainability are established together as the three pillars under Operational Priority 3, one of ADB's seven operational priorities to achieve its vision. To further the work on "do no harm" and "to do good," ADB's safeguards and environment group became separate divisions, with the latter focused on enhancing related knowledge, capacity, and investment projects in both public and private sectors.

Phase 3 (2023 onward): Enhancing environment portfolio to scale. With increased urgency to respond to global and regional environment challenges and learning from its past investments, under Phase 3 ADB is prepared to be more ambitious in scaling up its investments on environment and nature. From 2019 to 2023, total financing for ADB's environment-related portfolio was at $14.8 billion, with about 19% of the total tagged as enhancing environmental sustainability. In terms of type of projects, agriculture and natural resources accounted for 43% of the portfolio, followed by renewable energy and energy efficiency at 31%, finance at 13%, and others at 13%, which includes transport, public sector management, health, and water and urban infrastructure services (Figure 2). In terms of region, East Asia comprised the largest share of the portfolio with 34%, followed by Southeast Asia with 31%, South Asia with 19%, and Central and West Asia with 15%. The Pacific held less than 1% share. Regarding ADB's biodiversity portfolio, through an exercise conducted in 2021, there were an estimated 51 projects that support biodiversity conservation and restoration, with total financing of $1.65 billion, including $40 million in technical assistance (TA) projects. This is approximately 1.5% of ADB's loan portfolio.[29]

---

[27]   ADB. 2013. Environment Operational Directions 2013–2020.

[28]   Independent Evaluation Department. 2016. Environmentally Sustainable Growth: A Strategic Review. ADB.

[29]   ADB total portfolio was $133.9 billion at end 2021. ADB Financial Statements.

It is important to note that there are major limitations in determining ADB's environmental portfolio, with limited data tracking and monitoring system. The system is currently being assessed and planned to be updated with the ongoing review of the corporate results framework and other exercises. The tagging system on environment projects is currently limited to 15 subsectors under 3 sector groups at ADB, i.e., agriculture, food, nature and rural development energy, and finance sectors. As such, under the current system, environment-related investment in other sectors such as water and urban development, and transport are not systematically tagged and monitored. For instance, projects with air quality benefits, features, and/or components are not captured and reported unless they are dedicated air quality improvement projects. This is consistent with the Clean Air Fund study reporting that financiers do not fully account for the air quality benefits generated by their investments.[30]

Moreover, the project amount reflects the total value of the related projects and does not reflect the investment made on specific environment related components and activities. The total investment on environment related activities is significantly less, as many projects include components that are not specific to environment sustainability, such as costs for infrastructure development. Without a proper tracking and monitoring system on environment related projects and components, there are issues regarding the availability of data to accurately reflect current and planned financing for the environment. Reflecting on the Strategy 2030 MTR of ADB's Operational Priority 3 under and the joint initiative among the MDBs in tracking nature positive investments, work is underway to enhance the indicators and the tracking systems.

ADB will build on the lessons, experience and its gains from the initial years of Strategy 2030 implementation to ramp up the expansion and upscale its environment and nature portfolio. Building on the global momentum to urgently address nature and climate change challenges and following enhanced commitment among the MDBs to increase nature positive investment and mainstream nature into their operations, ADB will raise its profile on environment and nature in its investment portfolio. To do so, it will improve the enabling institutional environments not only of its clients, but also within ADB itself. (see Appendix 2: SWOT Analysis on Environment Actions in ADB Operations) As outlined in the next chapters, interventions will include removing institutional barriers; mobilizing resources; building systems, technological and technical capacities; establishing meaningful corporate monitoring and reporting systems; and cultivating strategic and knowledge partnerships.

---

[30]   Clean Air Fund. The State of Global Air Quality Funding 2023.

Figure 3: Environment-Related Portfolio at ADB, 2019–2023

Total finance: **$14.8 billion (14%)**

Proportion of projects: **19%**

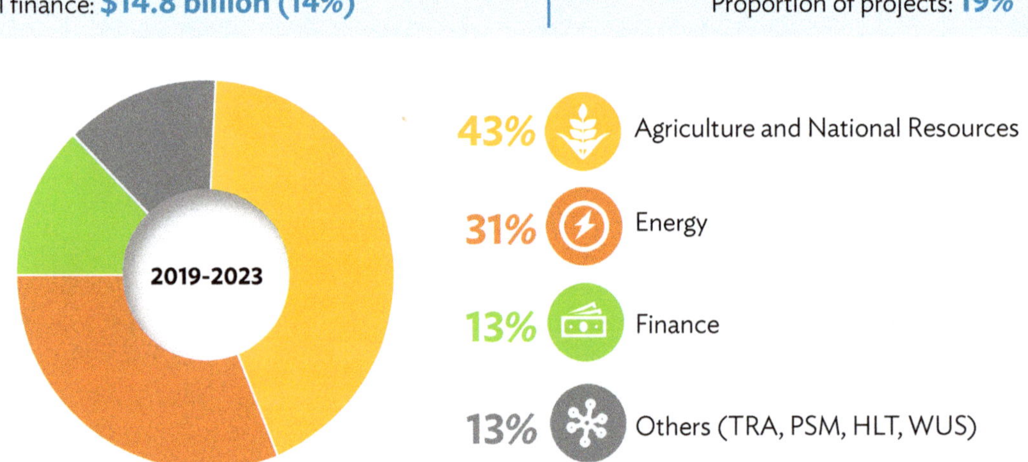

Note: Data is limited to only 3 Sectors and 15 Subsectors, due to the limited tracking under the OP3. This data is based on commitments. The amount captured reflects total value of the related projects and the actual project components specific to the environment likely form only a portion of the stated proportions.

ADB = Asian Development Bank; HLT = health; PSM = public sector management; TRA = transport; WUS = water and other urban infrastructure services.

Note: The 15 subsectors auto-tagged to Operational Priority 3–Pillar 3 on Enhancing Environmental Sustainability include (1) rural flood protection, (2) rural solid waste management, (3) fishery, (4) forestry, (5) land-based natural resources management, (6) water-based natural resources management, (7) renewable energy generation – solar, (8) renewable energy generation – wind, (9) renewable energy generation - biomass and waste, (10) renewable energy generation - small hydro, (11) renewable energy generation – geothermal, (12) energy efficiency and conservation, (13) insurance and contractual savings, (14) money and capital markets, and (15) infrastructure finance and investment funds.

Source: ADB Data.

II DIRECTIONS

Outcomes and Objectives

The EAP puts forth the why, what, and how of ADB's efforts to address the triple planetary crisis of biodiversity loss, increasing pollution, and climate change; and aims to expand the scope and scale of ADB's related investments with partners. The overall approach and vision of the EAP is guided by the theory of change as provided in Figure 4.

Figure 4: Theory of Change

Impact	Enhanced biodiversity and ecosystem management, reduced pollution, and enhanced climate action through nature-based solutions addressing the triple crisis

Outcome	Environmental sustainability is enhanced	Climate change mitigation is supported	Resilience against climate and disaster impacts is bolstered

Output	Enhanced capacity of ADB and DMC personnel for environmental sustainability programs	Increased ADB funding for nature-positive projects	Enhanced digital platforms for monitoring and managing ecosystems	Increased number of projects with nature-positive outcomes
	Development of new financial instruments	Improved institutional frameworks and coordination mechanisms at country and regional levels	Comprehensive databases and tools for ecosystem services valuation	Increased private sector participation in environmental projects

Key Activities

UPSTREAM	MIDSTREAM	DOWNSTREAM
• Integrate environmental sustainability into country partnership strategies and regional plans • Strengthen environmental governance by improving policies, laws, and regulations • Enhance key operational and business framework and processes	• Identify and integrate environmental concerns into project pipelines, public finances management, and procurement • Conduct regional diagnostic studies and prioritize nature-positive investment projects • Promote cross-sector coordination, regional cooperation, and innovative finance for environmental sustainability • Promote the integration of ecosystem services and natural capital into economic valuation of projects	• Increase the quantity and quality of projects aimed at reducing biodiversity loss and pollution • Integrate environmental sustainability features beyond safeguards in investment and procurement • Develop and leverage innovative financial instruments to support nature-positive investments • Provide technical inputs and design support for investment projects with NBS components.

CROSS-CUTTING

Partnerships and stakeholder engagement	Capacity building and training	Knowledge generation and sharing	Digital technologies and aritficial intelligence

Cause and Bariers	Unsustainable activities, weak environmental policies, market failures, insufficient awareness and capacity, and socio-economic pressures including population growth, urbanization, and poverty.

Problem Statement	Asia and the Pacific faces a triple crisis of biodiversity loss, pollution, and climate change, driven by unsustainable activities, weak policies, low valuation of ecosystem services, and socio-economic pressures, threatening sustainable development.

Source: ADB.

The EAP builds on the experience gained from past investments and implementing the Environmental Operational Directions from 2013–2020, and addresses the findings and recommendations from the Strategy 2030 Midterm Review and its five strategic focus areas.[31] The EAP promotes the One ADB approach and contributes to the four shifts in its operation: climate change, private sector, solutions-orientation, and new ways of working. It also brings together internal expertise and external partnerships to prioritize the most pressing issues across the triple planetary crisis The EAP will be implemented over the period 2024–2030, coinciding with the timeline of ADB's Strategy 2030.

As Asia and the Pacific's climate bank, ADB is uniquely placed among development organizations to address and support the process of placing the region's development onto a nature-positive and sustainable path. ADB is recognized as a trusted development organization with long standing relationships with its DMCs and regional stakeholders. This puts ADB in the position of being able to convene multiple DMCs and development partners and foster regional cooperation on priority issues such as environment and nature. Further, ADB offers a wide range of financing modalities for both sovereign and nonsovereign investments. Some of these modalities such as policy-based loans are recognized as particularly suitable for nature-positive investments. In addition, ADB is well experienced in leveraging financing from development partners, philanthropies, and green funds such as the Global Environment Facility, Global Climate Fund, and Climate Investment Fund. Finally, environmental actions are mainstreamed within ADB's sector operations and consistent with key sector priorities such as renewable energy, low-carbon transport, regenerative agriculture, green cities, and others. The strong and expanded sector operations portfolio related to environment and nature presents many opportunities for scaling up investment in environment and nature projects.

The EAP makes the case for ADB's expanded role in supporting its DMCs in addressing the major environmental challenges that the region is currently facing. The plan calls for linking environment and nature finance directly to ADB's role as the region's climate bank, recognizing the potential to generate wide-ranging benefits linked to climate change, biodiversity, and sustainable development. It is expected that upscaling of environment and nature finance in sector investments will substantively contribute to achieving ADB's intent to invest $100 billion in climate finance between 2019 to 2030.

The EAP seeks to align ADB's operations with key multilateral environmental agreements and strategies, including the Kunming–Montreal Global Biodiversity Framework, the Paris Agreement, and the upcoming Global Plastic Treaty. To add, the EAP operationalizes ADB's commitment under the *Joint Statement by the Multilateral Development Banks: Nature, People and Planet,* where MDBs affirmed their commitment to mainstreaming nature into their operations.

The EAP will serve as part of the series of action plans that is developed to strengthen ADB's operation on environment, climate change, and disaster risk management. ensure a holistic approach to addressing the interconnected challenges of climate change, disaster risk management, and environment and nature, driving progress toward a more prosperous, inclusive, resilient, and sustainable future (Box 5).

---

[31] Key recommendations of the MTR included (i) fostering the integration of environmental sustainability into DMCs' strategic planning, development, and investment decision making process; (ii) strengthening mainstreaming of environmental sustainability in ADB sector operations; (iii) supporting DMCs to deliver on global environmental commitments; (iv) supporting DMCs to transition to a circular economy and strengthen pollution control; (v) designing integrated solutions for climate action, nature conservation and protection, and sustainable land and water management; (vi) mainstreaming measurement and valuation of natural capital; (vii) revisiting the corporate results framework indicators and subsector mapping on environmental sustainability; (viii) expanding environmental sustainability tagging outside the framework; (ix) strengthening monitoring of environmental sustainability priorities and projects; and (x) catalyzing environment sustainability knowledge management.

Box 5: Relationship Between the Climate Change Action Plan, Disaster Risk Management Action Plan, and the Environment Action Plan

The series of three action plans—the Climate Change Action Plan approved in 2023, Disaster Risk Management Action Plan approved in 2024, and the environment action plan—provide a coordinated approach to addressing climate change, disaster risk management, and environmental management. These plans will work in harmony through (i) integrated planning and implementation, (ii) complementary financing and investments, (iii) coordinated capacity development initiatives, (iv) knowledge management and communication efforts, and (v) synergies in monitoring and reporting. Simultaneously, each plan addresses issues unique to its domain that are not addressed by the others, for example management of pollution and waste under the EAP, and geophysical hazards and post-disaster recovery under the DRMAP.

Source: ADB.

ADB will build on its client-centered and demand-driven approaches, and promote differentiated methods based on the capacity and interest of the countries in tackling environment and nature issues. As recommended by the Strategy 2030 MTR and considering the overall investment volume and potential for environmental impacts, ADB will bolster mainstreaming environment and nature in agriculture, food, nature and rural development; energy; and transport, while continuing to work on all sectors. The midterm review has also recognized growth areas for nature-positive investments in circular economy, nature-based solutions, and biodiversity conservation.

ADB will engage and empower vulnerable populations, including Indigenous Peoples and local communities, women and youth, and participate in decision-making processes and project design, implementation, and monitoring. Special attention will be made to augment inclusive approaches in addressing the environmental crisis, particularly by enhancing engagement with CSOs, including Indigenous Peoples, women's groups, and youth organizations. This recognizes the intergenerational aspects of environmental impacts and the potential of young people as agents of change in their communities.

There will be improved efforts to increase the environment portfolio in small island developing states, including in the Pacific region, and mountainous countries considering their vulnerability to climate change and biodiversity loss, while recognizing the wide diversity of national and regional contexts and taking differentiated approaches. The succeeding sections will further describe in detail how ADB intends to deliver environment operations at scale under an inclusive approach.

ADB's Environment Approach

ADB seeks to take a holistic approach to enhance nature-positive and mainstreaming approaches, and to upscale environment and nature finance within its operation. It aims to expand the scope and scale of investments, enhance the stewardship of natural capital, and accelerate actions for addressing biodiversity loss and ecosystem degradation, pollution, and climate change. Accordingly, both nature-positive and mainstreaming activities in projects and policies will be promoted under the following three interconnected and mutually reinforcing pillars (Figure 5):

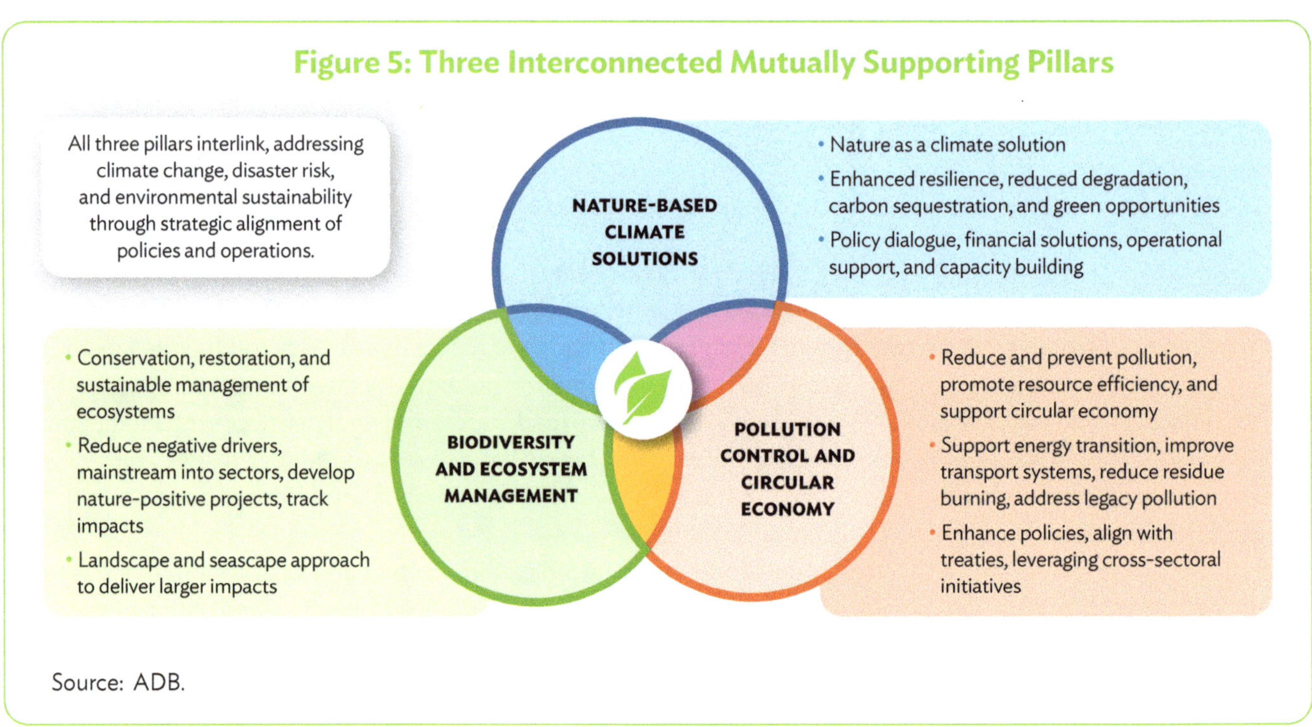

Pillar 1: Biodiversity and Ecosystem Management. This pillar will focus on conservation, restoration, and sustainable management of terrestrial and aquatic (including marine and freshwater) biodiversity and ecosystems. It will cover specific actions to deliver on ADB's commitments under the *MDB Joint Statement on Nature, People and Planet* and support DMC's commitment to implement their National Biodiversity Strategy and Action Plan and fulfill their commitments under the Kunming–Montreal Global Biodiversity Framework. It will include efforts to (i) reduce negative drivers for biodiversity loss across the portfolio; (ii) mainstream biodiversity friendly and ecosystem-based approaches into agriculture, food, nature, and rural development (including fisheries and aquaculture), infrastructure, energy, urban and water, and other sector project investments; (iii) develop nature-positive investments such as wildlife management and sustainable tourism development that directly benefit the economy and environment; and (iv) monitor, track, and disclose nature-positive and negative impacts and outcomes. Activities under this pillar will be embedded in investments in all sectors that ADB is engaged in. There will be enhanced collaboration with the agriculture, food, nature, and rural development sectors based on its investment portfolio that is mainly focused on natural resources management. Additionally, this pillar will integrate climate resilience and disaster risk reduction measures, recognizing that healthy ecosystems are vital for mitigating climate impacts and enhancing community resilience against natural hazards. Recognizing and respecting rights-based approaches on land and natural resources use, this pillar will work closely with Indigenous Peoples and local communities where relevant.

Given that key biodiversity areas are located across larger landscapes and seascapes, often beyond national boundaries, relevant nature investments will be identified and designed in a programmatic manner, where individual projects will be coordinated and linked to one another with a view to deliver larger impacts at a regional scale. Such an approach is currently being followed under the Regional Flyway Initiative and Ocean and Coastal Resilience Program

(Box 6). Building on these experiences, ADB will upscale and replicate biodiversity and ecosystem management at local, national, and regional scales with partners, including governments, private sector, CSOs, Indigenous Peoples, and local communities, and thereby through these initiatives contribute to regional environmental public goods. Specifically, in the Pacific Islands and small island developing states, these efforts will focus on enhancing marine and coastal ecosystem resilience, promoting sustainable tourism, and supporting community-based conservation initiatives.

Box 6: Ocean Resilience and Coastal Adaptation Trust Fund

Neighbors helping each other pull a fishing net in Gentuma Raya, Gorontalo, Indonesia (photo by ADB).

As a financial vehicle to scale its Ocean and Coastal Resilience Program, ADB established the Ocean Resilience and Coastal Adaptation Trust Fund (ORCA TF) in 2023 to promote climate-resilient and nature-positive sustainable development in coastal ecosystems across the Asia and Pacific region. With $13 million in initial grants from the Nordic Development Fund and the UK Foreign, Commonwealth, and Development Office, ORCA TF supports upstream planning, project preparation, and capacity development for investments in ocean health and coastal adaptation. In its first year, the fund mobilized $4.45 million for six technical assistance and grant activities, including a project to strengthen resilient and sustainable urban and water service delivery in the Pacific. The ORCA TF focuses on enhancing ocean health and resilience through nature-based solutions, ecosystem management and restoration, promoting a circular economy for plastic-free oceans, and supporting sustainable livelihoods for coastal communities. Key outcomes include improved ecosystem resilience, reduced marine plastic pollution, and strengthened community capacity for climate adaptation, demonstrating the fund's significant impact on biodiversity and environmental sustainability.

Source: ADB. Funds and Resources: Ocean Resilience and Coastal Adaptation Trust Fund.

Pillar 2: Pollution Control and Circular Economy. This pillar will focus on prevention, reduction, and management of environmental pollution, and promotion of efficient resource use. ADB will promote circular economy approaches and specific interventions for air quality, chemicals and waste, and water and marine pollution. Air quality improvements will build on past successful operations including work in the People's Republic of China[32] and Mongolia (Box 7).[33] Efforts will be made to address individual pollution challenges, while clearly identifying and leveraging cross-sector and regional initiatives to maximize positive outcomes at scale. This will include activities to promote better air quality through energy transition, improve transport systems, reduce agriculture residue burning, and others. On chemicals and waste, activities will include improvement in waste management, reduction of plastics and waste to marine debris, and promotion of a circular economy with efficient resource use among industries and communities. ADB will also support remediation of legacy pollution involving contaminated manufacturing and disposal sites, improving national and subnational policies and regulations for pollution management, and aligning to and implementing global and regional agreements and treaties on pollution management.

ADB will seek to scale up investments on addressing pollution and promoting resource use efficiency in sovereign and nonsovereign investments across multiple sectors and regions through (among others) mainstreaming circular economy approaches and resource use efficiency in sector investments, and leveraging financing for pollution prevention and management through innovative financing including by engaging the private sector (Box 8).

Box 7: Air Quality Improvement Programs

a. Beijing–Tianjin–Hebei region, the People's Republic of China

To improve the air quality in the People's Republic of China's major cities, ADB has invested a total of $2.55 billion between 2015 and 2020 through a series of loans comprising of one policy-based loan (PBL), five financial intermediary loans, one results-based lending, and one project loan. The mix of financing modalities was tailored to the needs of various kinds of activities and subprojects. The program was cofinanced by development partners such as KfW, World Bank, African Development Bank, the Green Climate Fund, and local commercial banks. The loans followed a programmatic, cross-sector, and cascading approach within the Beijing–Tianjin–Hebei region. The first few loans were targeted at strengthening the policy and regulatory framework on air quality including the establishment of a green financing platform. The program not only invested in large infrastructure projects like clean heating and gas pipelines targeted at highly polluted provinces, but also provided support to small and medium-sized enterprises (SMEs) and energy service companies that play a significant role in energy sector. The green financing platform which was the first of its kind was supported through financial intermediary loans. The platform provided sub-loans to help SMEs to switch to using clean energy systems and at the same time leverage private investments. A significant change in air pollution and carbon emissions resulted from the projects and enterprises: by 2022, there was a reduction of about 40% of particulate matter (PM2.5), 74% of sulfur dioxide, and 37% of nitrous oxides in comparison to 2015 levels.

continued on next page

---

[32]   ADB. 2015. *Report and Recommendation of the President to the Board of Directors: Proposed Policy-based Loan to the People's Republic of China for the Beijing-Tianjin-Hebei Air Quality Improvement Program*.

[33]   ADB. 2019. *Report and Recommendation of the President to the Board of Directors: Proposed Policy-based Loan and Technical Assistance Grant to Mongolia for the Ulaanbaatar Air Quality Improvement Program – Phase 2*.

Box 7 continued

b. Ulaanbaatar, Mongolia

ADB aimed to address severe air pollution in Ulaanbaatar, Mongolia, through a two-phase Ulaanbaatar Air Quality Improvement Program, implemented between March 2018 and December 2020, using PBLs. Phase 1 and Phase 2 were supported by $130 million and $160 million in loans respectively, aimed at (i) improving air quality management; (ii) adopting urgent air pollution reduction measures; and (iii) establishing environmentally sound urban, energy, and transport systems. Key activities included the approval of the National Program for Reducing Air and Environmental Pollution, distributing 80,000 tons of less polluting briquettes, and piloting the pneumococcal conjugate vaccine for 40,000 people. Furthermore, air quality monitoring standards were improved, onsite coal-fired heat-only boilers were prohibited in new public buildings, and a 20-year master plan was prepared for Ulaanbaatar. This led to a 46% reduction in average winter PM2.5 concentrations compared to 2016–2017 levels, improved public health, and heightened awareness of cleaner energy practices. The program strengthened regulatory frameworks to address air pollution and promoted sustainable urban planning. This program in Mongolia exemplifies how PBLs can effectively tackle air pollution, providing a model for other cities facing similar challenges.

Source: ADB. People's Republic of China: Beijing-Tianjin-Hebei Air Quality Improvement-Hebei Policy Reforms Program; Ulaanbataar Air Quality Improvement Program; Ulaanbataar Air Quality Improvement Program – Phase 2.

Box 8: Promoting a Circular Economy for Plastics in Indonesia

Indonesia is among the largest contributors of marine debris globally, with 350,000 tons of plastic waste discharged into the marine environment each year. To help the country meet its marine debris reduction goals, ADB is supporting a holistic and system-wide approach to enable and operationalize a circular economy for plastics. Approved in May 2024, ADB is investing $500 million in a policy-based lending program with cofinancing partners Agence Française de Developpement and KfW to support government policy reforms to improve plastic waste management, reduce problematic plastic production and consumption, and strengthen data and monitoring tools for policy making. This is complemented by technical assistance

Enabling a circular economy. ADB is helping reduce plastic pollution in Indonesia by engaging the plastics value chain to develop circular economy solutions, such as improved waste management and recycling (photo by Victor Beaumont).

to develop road maps for digitalizing the plastics value chain and city-level plastic circularity. ADB has also invested in infrastructure for plastics circularity, including $144 million in blue loans to Indorama Ventures Ltd and PT Alba Tridi to expand its plastic bottle recycling capacity and a $450,000 grant to Alner, an Indonesian social venture, to pilot its reusable packaging and refilling solution for consumer goods. This comprehensive package of sovereign and private sector investments will support a system-wide transition to a circular plastics economy, providing a replicable model for enabling circularity in other countries and sectors.

Source: ADB. Indonesia: Reducing Marine Debris Program, Subprogram 1; Indorama Ventures Regional Blue Loan Project; and Alba Blue Loan for Recycling.

Pillar 3: Nature-based Climate Solutions. Investing in nature can enhance community resilience and adaptation capacities, prevent environmental degradation, support carbon sequestration and storage, and open greener economic opportunities, while significantly contributing to disaster risk management by reducing the impacts of disasters caused by natural hazards. Hence, this pillar will promote nature-based solutions to address climate change, biodiversity loss, and pollutions, including addressing water and food insecurities by protecting, restoring, and managing natural capital and ecosystem services. Following a programmatic approach, this pillar will promote nature-based climate solutions through a combination of (i) designing and implementing policies and regulations, tools, guidance, and other sector instruments that enable nature-based solutions at the national and regional level; (ii) integrating nature-based solutions into investment projects; (iii) financial and technical advisory services through the Nature Solutions Finance Hub by preparing bankable projects using innovative finance instruments and increased revenue streams to enable scale; (iv) operational support through project design clinics and technical inputs to improve the design of investment projects with nature-based solutions components; and (v) knowledge and capacity building through publications, seminars, and trainings.

All three pillars are closely interlinked, have direct influence on, and are affected by climate change mitigation and adaptation and disaster risk management. Environmental pollution and inefficient resource use result in biodiversity loss and ecosystem degradation and reduce the effectiveness of nature-based solutions (Box 9) for addressing climate change and disaster risk management. Similarly, biodiversity loss and ecosystem degradation exacerbate pollution and waste issues by reducing the natural capacity to filter and absorb pollutants, which diminish the effectiveness of nature-based solutions and weaken ecosystems' resilience and sequestration potential, thereby increasing vulnerability and hindering climate mitigation efforts.

On the other hand, climate change as well as disasters triggered by natural hazards and anthropogenic causes have devastating impacts on environment and nature, including significant loss of biodiversity, habitat destruction, soil erosion, water scarcity, and degradation of ecosystems. Therefore, in line with the climate change action plan and disaster risk management action plan, the environment action plan also intends to implement upstream strategic engagement for enhanced policy and regulatory frameworks, embed environmental actions in core institutions and national systems at the midstream level, and ensure high-quality operations and implementation downstream.

Box 9: Nature-Based Solutions and Nature-Positive Finance

Nature-based solutions are defined as "actions to protect, conserve, restore, sustainably use and manage natural or modified terrestrial, freshwater, coastal and marine ecosystems which address social, economic and environmental challenges effectively and adaptively, while simultaneously providing human well-being, ecosystem services, resilience and biodiversity benefits" (UNEA 2022). Examples of nature-based solutions include bioengineering, wetland management, and river-basin management.

Nature-positive finance—as defined and agreed among the multilateral development banks under the Common Principles for tracking nature-positive finance—refers to finance that supports actions that protect, restore or enhance sustainable use and management of nature, or enables these actions and contributes to the implementation of the Kunming–Montreal Global Biodiversity Framework and its broad ambition to halt and reverse nature loss by 2030, with a view to full recovery by 2050. Such an action must also meet all the following eligibility criteria, as determined by the respective MDB:

- makes a substantive contribution to nature;
- has expected positive outcomes for nature that are measurable and can be assessed and monitored against a baseline, where feasible, or otherwise, a business-as-usual scenario; and
- is not expected to introduce significant adverse environmental risks or impacts.

The definition of nature-positive finance encompasses the following relevant activity types: Protection refers to those activities that maintain the status and condition of biodiversity and ecosystems.

- Restoration refers to the process of assisting the recovery of an ecosystem that has been degraded, damaged or destroyed relative to a reference state.
- Sustainable use and management of nature indicates a shift of economic activity away from processes driving nature loss.
- Enabling conditions refer to policies, models and sectoral instruments, incentives, data, and other tools enabling the above activities.

Source: United Nations Environment Assembly of the United Nations Environment Program Fifth Session; MDB Common Principles for tracking nature-positive finance.

III OPERATIONALIZATION

ADB will engage in upstream, midstream, downstream, and crosscutting actions to develop the required enabling environment and enhance and scale the investments on environment and nature across all ADB operations. This will cover, (i) upstream engagements to redefining priorities and refining environmental diagnostics across DMCs and regions, sharing and generating knowledge on priority and emerging environment and nature-related issues, and ensuring strategic integration of environmental priorities into country partnership strategies; (ii) midstream actions in identifying policy and regulatory measures to create an enabling environment, integrating environment priorities into ADB programming exercises, and developing a pipeline of projects; and (iii) downstream actions to implementing needed assessments and studies, and developing and implementing both public and private sector investments. The EAP has also identified four cross-cutting measures across the three streams, including stakeholder engagements, knowledge sharing, capacity development, and digital technologies. The following section provides an overview of the approach that will be taken for operationalizing the EAP following the theory of change provided in Figure 4, while action items are specified in Appendix 1.

Upstream Engagement

Participating in country partnership strategies. The assessment processes and the dialogue with the country stakeholders leading up to ADB's country partnership strategies (CPS) constitute an important opportunity to address key environmental issues, following government development priorities, institutions, capacities, and existing or planned programs, as well as recent lessons and trends in the country. ADB will review and update existing guidance and promote integrated environmental assessments and diagnostic work into the CPS preparation process, including overview assessment of the state of the environment, covering biodiversity and natural resource management, pollution, climate change, and disaster risk management. These will be closely coordinated with assessments carried out to fulfill safeguard requirements. This exercise will help identify critical environmental constraints and challenges, support the mapping of natural capital, and integrate valuation of ecosystem goods and services into economic planning processes, including piloting the use of alternative wealth indexes that incorporate environmental and social values distinct from GDP, to ensure CPS' development support and program interventions that can lead to environmentally resilient, low-carbon, and sustainable economic growth. Natural capital accounting and valuation can play a key role in conceptualizing nature as assets worth restoring, maintaining, and enhancing in the DMCs with productive economic and social value (Box 10).

Box 10: Natural Capital Accounting and Ecosystem Services Valuation

Integrating ecosystem services valuation into the economic analysis of ADB projects promotes environmental considerations and becomes integral to assessing economic development projects. The bank's Economic Research and Development Impact Department undertakes analytical and methodological research to improve economic analysis of ADB project investments as well as provide advisory services and capacity building to support operations for greater development effectiveness. In this light, a guidebook is being prepared to provide an extensive overview of best practices, approaches, and methods for measuring and integrating the monetary value of ecosystem services into economic project analyses. In addition, ADB is developing an ecosystem services value tool to systematically collect nonmarket values of various ecosystems to facilitate integration of ecosystem values at project design and during quality at entry stage of project economic assessments. Moreover, in collaboration with Stanford University's Natural Capital Lab, ADB is piloting natural capital assessment and accounting initiatives in the People's Republic of China, Armenia, the Philippines, Sri Lanka, and Cook Islands.

Source: Asian Development Bank.

Through this process, ADB will assist DMCs in aligning their policies, plans, and investments with global biodiversity targets and help them prepare, strengthen, and implement their national biodiversity strategies and action plans, along with the nationally determined contributions on climate change and other global commitments. The process will employ integrated spatial planning tools and effective management processes to prioritize the protection of important biodiversity areas, while ensuring gender mainstreaming and respecting the rights of and engaging Indigenous Peoples and local communities. Additionally, ADB will integrate sustainable procurement practices into the CPS preparation process, encouraging the use of nature-based solutions and assessing the nature impact of supply chains to ensure that procurement decisions across projects are not only aligned with but also actively promote environmental sustainability goals.

Enhancing key operational and business framework and processes, including monitoring systems. ADB will update the environmental sustainability outcome indicators and incorporate ADB's corporate results framework to accurately reflect the contribution of ADB's nature-positive and mainstreaming pipeline, and establish key impact metrics and a monitoring system for environmental programs under the three pillars of the EAP. These impact metrics will be aligned with key global commitments such as the Kunming–Montreal Global Biodiversity Framework, SDGs, and the MDB Common Principles for Tracking Nature-Positive Finance, and will support reporting against future standards such as the Taskforce on Nature-related Financial Disclosures. ADB will also explore updating its Project Classification System and Sovereign Operations systems for accurate accounting of sectors and sub-sectors with nature positive and/or environmentally sustainable activities/components. The revised Project Classification System will support operationalization of the "MDB Common Principles for tracking nature-positive finance" and track projects related to biodiversity and ecosystem management, nature-based solutions, and pollution management and circular economy. ADB will prepare internal guidance for tagging environment and nature investments to support implementation of the revised project classification system and sovereign operations systems. This will also include guidance on entry points and approaches for promoting environment and nature finance in sector investments. Finally, ADB will explore designing a financial incentives framework to encourage and support environment and nature investments in the DMCs.

Midstream Engagement

Supporting related policies and regulations. ADB will continue supporting DMCs to strengthen environmental governance. This will include refining environmental policies, laws, and regulations to meet international best practices, improving on their implementation and enforcement, and strengthening institutional coordination and capacity for environmental management and protection. Through harmonization with the CCAP, DRMAP,and other closely linked policies and strategies such as the new environmental and social framework for safeguards, ADB will also support DMCs with the preparation of policy and regulatory reforms to address environmental and climate change challenges using approaches such as market-based instruments, incentives for environmentally sustainable practices, and, where appropriate, conducting strategic environmental assessments for national, subnational, regional, transboundary and sector planning. Furthermore, ADB will assist DMCs in strengthening policy and regulatory frameworks to promote synergy between nature conservation, climate mitigation efforts, and sustainable natural resource management. This method will integrate nature-related financial disclosures, green public financial management, and sustainable procurement into project designs and supportive policies, ensuring that both public and private activities and financial flows are aligned with nature-positive approaches and SDGs. Policy-based loans also provide ADB with a platform to engage in a comprehensive dialogue with governments on key environmental policies and legislation. Upstream policy reforms and actions can be paired with initiatives that prioritize nature-positive outcomes and the mainstreaming of environment in relevant programming and investments. Efforts will be undertaken to frontload specific diagnostics and knowledge products in a growing number of DMCs to ensure a high quality of policy dialogue under relevant policy-based loans.

Enhancing programming and technical support: ADB will actively engage with DMCs and the private sector to identify key environmental issues at the national and regional levels, and integrate environment, nature, and biodiversity concerns into the respective country's development planning and fiscal framework, public investment and budget framework, and ADB's programming exercises. This integration will focus on embedding environmental priorities and natural capital assessment and valuation within public finance management, national budgeting processes, and procurement to align strategic and fiscal frameworks with sustainability goals (Box 11).

Box 11: Green Public Financial Management

Green public financial management refers to the integration of a climate-friendly perspective into existing ADB programs, public financial management practices, systems, and frameworks. The objective is to promote fiscal policies that are responsive to environmental and climate concerns. It incorporates climate risk assessments into budget planning, monitoring, and execution. It helps identify vulnerabilities related to climate change and ensures that funds are allocated to mitigate these risks, by ensuring that budget allocations consider environment, nature, and climate-related priorities that promote sustainability. Budgets are evaluated based on environmental outcomes. Metrics related to emissions reduction, energy efficiency, and natural resource conservation can be tracked under an efficient green public financial management system to assess the effectiveness of green initiatives. Citizens can track how public funds are used for green projects, making environmental spending transparent and accountable.

Source: ADB. 2023. Green Public Investment Management: Governance Aspects of Strengthening Infrastructure Sustainability.

Given the regional and transboundary nature of key biodiversity, water resource management, and pollution challenges, these issues will be tackled through regional cooperation and integration technical assistance (TA) projects and investment projects. These projects will target key subregions or regional landscapes and seascapes. Support will be provided for conducting diagnostic studies for targeted regions and geographic units such as cities or provinces. One such example is the Nepal TA, which includes actions to strengthen biodiversity conservation and reduce pollution at the river basin. Such projects will enable the creation of a pipeline of nature-positive investment projects and/or sector-focused projects with strong environmental mainstreaming components. Support will also be provided to build the capacity of DMCs, including government, the private sector, CSOs, and local communities, for managing and monitoring environmental issues straddling multiple projects. In addition, given ADB's comparative advantage of being able to convene multiple stakeholders across many countries, ADB will facilitate dialogue and cooperation among DMCs facing regional biodiversity and pollution problems requiring transboundary cooperation and actions.

Box 12: River Ravi Eco-Revitalization Master Plan

The River Ravi Basin in Pakistan is home to 52 million people in the country's most populous province. Nearly 75% of the river basin is used for agriculture, helping feed millions of Pakistanis, and is a lifeline to families and businesses across urban and rural areas. It is highly deteriorated, i.e., 400% below the minimum quality to sustain aquatic life with high risk of water-borne diseases, threatening the health of basin residents.

The River Ravi Eco-Revitalization Master Plan developed with ADB support is a detailed road map for achieving the people's vision of "a tapestry of diverse, healthy river environments that nurture and support human well-being." It is a long-term, holistic, multisector plan to revitalize and build resilience in the river basin ecosystem and includes recommendations for investment projects, institutional reforms, and public–private partnerships (including community ownership). The plan has five main elements: (i) land demarcation and acquisition, (ii) wastewater treatments, (iii) integrated urban water management, (iv) awareness campaign, and (v) agricultural and industrial policies.

The plan employs an adaptive, phased approach. Phase 1 (5 to 10-year horizon) focuses on near-term opportunities demonstrating the possibilities to improve water access and quality treatment, ecological health, and recreational value. Phase 2 (20-year horizon) extends earlier work across the basin particularly in small urban *nullahs* and large dirty *nullahs*. Phase 3 (30-year horizon) envisages tertiary wastewater treatment in most parts of the basin and widespread restoration.

ADB helped prepare eight prefeasibility assessments for priority investments, including nature-based solutions for wastewater treatment and flood risk management in Faisalabad and Lahore regions. Moreover, a draft concept paper was prepared for the Reintegration and Revitalization of the River Ravi Project, and the proposed project is now included in the country's rolling pipeline for 2025–2027.

Note: Nullahs is the local term used for natural streams and drainage channels converted into open sewers over time.
Source: ADB. Pakistan's River Ravi Eco-Revitalization Master Plan.

Promoting innovative finance. To fill the large funding gap needed to reverse biodiversity loss and scale up nature finance, ADB will seek to innovate its range of financial instruments to maximize capital mobilization. This includes mobilizing funds through green and blue bonds as well as sustainability-linked bonds, and exploring biodiversity and nature bonds and credits, and debt-for-nature swaps. ADB, in collaboration with partners, will also promote designing projects with strong financial structure that increases revenue streams that could incentivize public and private sectors to further invest in environment and nature. ADB will also engage in fostering public–private partnerships (PPPs), leveraging private sector and CSO investments—including through high-integrity carbon markets—alongside public, donor, and philanthropic funds. ADB will promote the application of relevant digital technologies and innovative solutions in its financial products, and support nature-related financial disclosures. Initiatives such as the Nature Solutions Finance Hub can be expanded and replicated to serve not only nature-based solutions but also other environmental challenges such as air pollution and waste management. In addition, ADB will support DMCs in preparing long overdue reforms such as eliminating harmful subsidies, revising debt instruments, reforming economic incentives in the form of credits or tax relief, and mobilizing domestic resources. The EAP will align with the CCAP and DRMAP in leveraging innovative financing mechanisms—such as the green and blue financing initiatives mentioned in the CCAP—to maximize co-benefits among the different streams of work.

Promoting environmentally sustainable procurement. ADB will encourage the incorporation of environmental sustainability throughout procurement processes and supply chains of projects that it finances. This will be achieved by identifying high-impact areas, setting sustainability requirements and criteria, adopting green specifications and standards and whole-of-life costing, and promoting the adoption of digital solutions for smarter use of resources and low-impact infrastructure. The EAP will support the incorporation of environment criteria during strategic procurement planning and bidding for ADB-financed projects. Additionally, environmental considerations will be integrated into procurement due diligence and diagnostic assessments at the project and country levels. ADB will promote and support the incorporation of sustainable procurement practices in national public procurement frameworks through TA projects, policy-based lending, and knowledge partnerships. To enhance adoption over the entire infrastructure supply chain, ADB will collaborate with other international organizations, the private sector, training institutions, CSOs, and industries on business outreach and capacity building related to sustainable procurement.

Box 13: Sustainable Public Procurement

Since launching its Sustainable Public Procurement Guidance Note in 2021 overseen by the Procurement, Portfolio, and Financial Management Department, ADB continues to support increased sustainability in the projects it finances. ADB is promoting incorporation of sustainable procurement practices in national public procurement frameworks through technical assistance, policy-based lending, and knowledge partnerships. In September 2024 ADB launched a sustainable procurement hub that will provide both external and internal stakeholders with a knowledge platform on sustainable procurement. It includes process guidelines, sector and thematic specific references, case studies, country diagnostics, and key supply chain market reports. ADB is leading the MDB Heads of Procurement working group on sustainable procurement. The current focus of the workstreams is on carbon measurement, evaluation templates, and promotion of sustainable procurement.

Source: ADB. 2024. Sustainable Public Procurement Guidance Note; Joint Statement on Sustainable Procurement Initiatives by the Heads of Procurement at Multilateral Development Banks.

Promoting cross-sector integration and regional cooperation. In recognition of the interdependencies across sectors and opportunities for tackling multiple environmental challenges simultaneously, ADB will promote cross-sector coordination. For example, an emerging nexus approach to tackling air pollution, improving crop productivity, and promoting clean energy entails the diversion of crop residue away from burning and toward its use as fuel for power generation. By facilitating cross-pollination of ideas across different sectors, ADB aims to harness diverse expertise and drive innovation in nature-positive and mainstreaming projects. In addition, ADB will promote regional cooperation and collective action and build on existing regional cooperation programs such as the Central Asia Regional Economic Cooperation (CAREC) Program, Greater Mekong Subregion (GMS) Program, South Asia Subregional Economic Cooperation (SASEC) Program and other programs that ADB contributes to such as the Bay of Bengal Initiative for Multi-Sectoral Technical and Economic Cooperation, and the Association of Southeast Asian Nations. Through these programs, ADB will seek to mobilize resources at scale and support projects on transboundary air and water management, pollution control, coastal management, and regional energy grids, benefiting multiple countries and enhancing regional sustainability including knowledge exchange, technology transfer, alignment with relevant regional and global standards, and harmonized monitoring and management approaches. The recent endorsement of the Phnom Penh Joint Statement on Plastic Pollution Control demonstrates how subregional frameworks can drive significant environmental progress. Environment ministers from the countries in the GMS have pledged to collaboratively enhance policies, improve waste management infrastructure, promote research into sustainable alternatives to plastics, and advance community-based approaches to effectively combat plastic pollution across the region.

Downstream Engagement

Scaling nature positive investments. ADB will scale up the number, size, and quality of projects and programs that directly address biodiversity loss, pollution, and nature-based solutions as the main objectives. While ADB's portfolio on nature-positive investments is still limited with projects, there are increasing opportunities to expand the portfolio based on growing interest and needs by the DMCs and private sector. There is considerable potential for nature-based solutions to mitigate climate change and contribute to climate resilience and disaster risk reduction objectives. In this expansion, ADB will leverage climate finance for nature-positive investments and incorporate nature-based solutions and nature positive supply chains in project investment and related procurement processes (Box 13) to ensure that all activities align with broader environment and nature-positive approaches. Implementation of a green public financial management system at the national and subnational levels, adherence to sustainable financial reporting standards, and the incorporation of environmental, social, and governance considerations at project and organizational levels will be closely monitored and enforced.

ADB seeks to scale up such projects; expand the range of nature-positive investments by re-engaging in sectors such as forestry, agriculture, water resource management, aquaculture, and fisheries as recommended by the Strategy 2030 MTR of OP3; and explore new areas for investments. Examples of such projects include the Shaanxi Qinling Biodiversity Conservation and Demonstration Project, Indorama Ventures Blue Loan Project, Indonesia ALBA Blue Loan for Recycling, Cambodia Sustainable Coastal and Marine Fisheries Project, and the proposed Hunan Dongting Lake Wetland Restoration and Sustainable Development Project (Box 14).

Box 14: Regional Flyway Initiative and the PRC Hunan South Dongting Lake Wetland Restoration and Sustainable Development Project

Tundra Swans in South Dongting Lake Wetland (photo by the Hunan Government website).

The Hunan South Dongting Lake Wetland Restoration and Sustainable Development Project, managed by the Yuanjiang Municipal Government in Hunan Province, is an approximately $308 million environmental initiative which is financed with $150 million from ADB, $65 million from the Agence Française de Developpement, and about $93 million from government funds. This project marks ADB's first standalone project developed through the Regional Flyway Initiative (RFI) which is a partnership between ADB, the East Asian-Australasian Flyway Partnership, and Birdlife International. South Dongting Lake is one of the 23 highest priority inland wetland sites in the People's Republic of China (PRC) for migratory waterbirds. The project will demonstrate how adopting a landscape approach that links ecosystem restoration with sustainable livelihoods can also deliver wetland protection and migratory waterbird conservation. The project aims to enhance institutional capacity for wetland management at the landscape level, directly restore almost 12,000 hectares of degraded wetlands, create habitats for biodiversity and migratory birds, and improve climate-resilient livelihoods through about $20 million eco-compensation fund and through ecotourism development. The project also seeks to boost knowledge and capacity of local and regional stakeholders to share lessons and adapt strategies across other RFI sites in the PRC and the region.

Source: ADB. 2024. Hunan South Dongting Lake Wetland Restoration and Sustainable Development Project.

To expand nature-positive investment, ADB's Climate Change and Sustainable Development Department (CCSD) will collaborate closely with Sector Groups including agriculture, food, nature, and rural development as well as water and urban development, where the scope of investments often inherently involves biodiversity and natural resource management. Enhanced cooperation is also expected with the finance sector office as finance interventions, including innovative finance instruments, offer opportunities to leverage increased capital and improved results on nature-positive outcomes. ADB will promote the uptake of DMCs' nature-positive projects by supporting innovative financial instruments such as biodiversity and nature bonds, debt-for-nature swaps, and leveraging concessional or grant financing from cofinancers and biodiversity funds. Moreover, ADB will provide support in strengthening legal and regulatory frameworks to support nature-positive investments and provide advisory services to governments in designing and implementing nature-positive projects, including carbon projects (e.g., sequestration of blue carbon in coastal and marine ecosystems) and finding suitable offtake avenues to unlock additional financing from the carbon markets. Resources will be tapped from sovereign lending and financing facilities such as the Nature Solutions Finance Hub (Box 15, Innovative Finance Facility for Climate in Asia and the Pacific, and the Association of Southeast Asian Nations Catalytic Green Finance Facility to further leverage investments from cofinancers and the private sector. A list of nature-positive interventions that will be scaled up under the EAP is provided in Appendix 1, section C1.

Box 15: Nature Solutions Finance Hub

The Asian Development Bank (ADB) launched the Nature Solutions Finance Hub (NSFH) at COP 28 to address environmental challenges and promote nature-based solutions (NBS) among its developing member countries. The NSFH aims to catalyze at least $5 billion in capital flows for NBS projects—including private capital—by developing innovative finance models such as nature bonds, structures utilizing carbon credits, and blended finance mechanisms. Funded by ADB and its partners, the NSFH will enhance institutional capacities, create a pipeline of nature-positive projects, support project design and implementation, and establish knowledge exchange platforms to promote NBS. Key activities include creating a de-risking fund to enhance project bankability, conducting training programs for stakeholders, and setting up a Nature Bonds Incubator. This initiative aligns with global commitments like the Sustainable Development Goals, the Paris Agreement, and the Kunming–Montreal Global Biodiversity Framework. With its aim to scale up investments in NBS to combat climate change, biodiversity loss, and environmental degradation, the NSFH fosters sustainable development across Asia and the Pacific.

Source: ADB. 2024. Nature Solutions Finance Hub for Climate and the Environment.

Mainstream environmental sustainability into operations, investments, and procurement. ADB will enhance technical and financial support for integrating environment and nature mainstreaming activities beyond safeguards in both sovereign and nonsovereign investments under all sectors, including agriculture, food, nature and rural development, energy, finance, public sector management, social development, transport, water and urban development, and trade, including tourism. Projects under these sectors will be supported to further improve their design and incorporate actions and measures to reverse and restore natural resource depletion, biodiversity loss, pollution, and climate change; and complement environment safeguards and maximize opportunities for generating environmental and climate benefits. Most, if not all biodiversity protection and pollution reduction measures generate climate co-benefits such as enhance resilience and/or reducing greenhouse gases. Therefore, existing climate change-related incentives such as grants or concessional loans for projects will be leveraged also for purposes of integrating environment concerns and nature conservation in investment projects. Support will also be provided to facilitate relevant sector investments for conducting environment-related data collection, feasibility studies, diagnostic studies, policy dialogue, action planning, stakeholder mapping, and cost–benefit analysis for projects. Assessment and valuation of natural capital and ecosystem services in project economic analysis will be promoted to improve the consideration of nature and environment as part of the planning, design, execution, and evaluation of projects. Environment criteria and standards will be integrated into the procurement processes at project and country level, ensuring that all purchases support broader environmental goals and reduce ecological impact.

ADB will seek to replicate and scale up existing good practice and projects with strong nature-based solutions and environmental approaches including across key regions such as SASEC, CAREC, GMS, and others as mentioned above. Examples of such projects include Viet Nam Secondary Cities Green Development Program, Bangladesh South Asia Subregional Economic Cooperation Chittagong – Cox's Bazar Rail Project (Box 17), India Sustainable Coastal Protection and Management Investment Program, and PRC Jiangxi Rural–Urban Infrastructure Development Project (Box 17). A list of interventions for mainstreaming environment sustainability in sector investments is provided in Appendix 1, section C2.

Box 16: Nature-Based Solutions to Create Sponge Cities and Promote Integrated Rural–Urban Infrastructure

ADB has piloted the "sponge city" concept across 16 cities in the People's Republic of China (PRC) through the Jiangxi Pingxiang Integrated Rural-Urban Infrastructure Development Project. This initiative addresses severe flooding that has plagued Pingxiang since 1998, affecting over 496,000 people and causing significant agricultural and infrastructural damage. The project employs nature-based solutions such as floodplain protection, wetland rehabilitation, green embankments, public river greenways, and wetland parks to absorb, store, and gradually release rainwater. This approach not only mitigates flood risks but also enhances water management, biodiversity, and urban livability while being cost-effective. By incorporating green infrastructure, the sponge city model aims to recharge groundwater, harvest rainwater, minimize the urban impact on the natural water cycle, and improve wastewater treatment and collection, thereby promoting climate resilience and sustainable development. The successful implementation in Pingxiang, supported by a $150 million ADB loan and additional technical assistance, sets a precedent for other Asian cities to follow, highlighting the multifaceted benefits of nature-based solutions in creating resilient and sustainable urban environments.

Source: ADB. Jiangxi Pingxiang Integrated Rural-Urban Infrastructure Development Project.

Box 17: Biodiversity Conservation in the Chittagong–Cox's Bazar Green Rail Line Project

The Chittagong-Cox's Bazar Rail Project was approved by ADB in 2016 with a $1.5 billion loan. The project involves constructing a 103-kilometer green rail line from Dohazari to Cox's Bazar, which passes through three protected areas and multiple elephant corridors. To mitigate significant biodiversity impacts, ADB implemented innovative measures such as the world's first elephant overpass, multiple underpasses, and funnel fencing to guide elephants safely across the rail line. A habitat enhancement plan was implemented to ensure tree plantation and creation of salt licks and water holes, improving wildlife habitats. Additionally, pilot-tested sensor technology to prevent

World's first elephant overpass along the Chittagong–Cox's Bazar Railway Line, Bangladesh (photo by Jiang Yafei).

elephant-train collisions is being procured for full installation. These comprehensive strategies, aligned with ADB's Safeguard Policy Statement, demonstrate a science-based, data-driven approach to integrating ecological preservation into infrastructure development, ensuring the protection of endangered species and their habitats while advancing sustainable transportation infrastructure.

Source: ADB. South Asia Subregional Economic Cooperation Chittagong-Cox's Bazar Railway Project, Phase 1.

Crosscutting Measures

Enhancing partnerships. ADB has built strong partnerships with many multilateral and bilateral donors, private sector firms, international and national CSOs, research institutions, think tanks, and expert groups over the past decades in promoting and implementing environment and nature-related projects. ADB will continue to strengthen these partnerships and strategically make new ones. This will be enhanced with a view to exchanging knowledge on best practices and technical expertise, mobilizing financing, and combining efforts to support DMCs in addressing key environmental issues based on national context. Partnership with relevant regional and subregional economic cooperation programs is also important to increase impact and sustainability of the initiatives.[34] In addition, ADB will promote inclusivity by engaging in participatory consultations, implementation and monitoring; providing targeted capacity building; and implementing tailored interventions by applying gender and social inclusion frameworks to enhance both social equity and ecological outcomes. It will involve a broader spectrum of stakeholders in every stage of project management to ensure diverse perspectives and needs are considered, thereby enhancing the sustainability and acceptance of projects.

Enhancing private sector engagement. Fostering partnerships with the private sector is critical in reducing the financial gap to address pressing environment degradation and nature loss. Collaboration with the private sector will leverage necessary expertise, technology, and capital in projects focused on the environment. ADB will explore novel financing mechanisms that involve private investment in resilience-building, nature-positive investments, and nature-based solutions. Engagement with private sector entities is particularly important to reduce the financial gap in addressing pressing environmental issues, promote sustainable financing for nature-positive investments, and

---

[34] Regional and subregional economic cooperation programs such as the GMS, CAREC, and SASEC can be useful platforms to address cross-border environmental issues.

catalyze private sector capital and investment. For example, private sector investment, particularly by insurance companies and financial institutions, can boost environment and nature-related investments by developing unique financial products such as green and blue bonds, sustainability-linked loans, and climate risk insurance, and by investing in projects that support positive actions with nature.

Engaging with stakeholders. ADB will actively engage with key stakeholders such as government agencies, the private sector, academia, CSOs, including Indigenous Peoples and local communities, women and youth groups, and people with disabilities to collaborate and enhance environment and nature investment in ADB operations. Engagement with CSOs, Indigenous Peoples and local communities will be enhanced in identifying and managing relevant programs and investments. These collaborations will be vital for integrating diverse perspectives and expertise in the design, implementation, and monitoring of development projects. CSOs will play a pivotal role in bridging gaps between local stakeholders and enhancing the development effectiveness of ADB's operations. Their technical expertise in environmental management will be crucial for promoting good governance, accountability, and sustainability in environmental projects. ADB will enhance engagement with Indigenous Peoples and local communities in applying inclusive nature-based solutions and their environment and nature practices nested on their traditional knowledge. Stakeholder engagement will be conducted by following strong gender responsive approach and promote gender equality and women's empowerment.

Enhancing knowledge generation and sharing. ADB will continue its efforts to generate knowledge on environmental issues, nature-based solutions, and related practices, focusing on integrating the latest scientific advances and technological innovations, and application and policy uses of natural capital assessment and ecosystem valuation. To address the gaps in current knowledge sharing systems, ADB will harness and integrate existing tools, networks, and expertise to ensure interoperability and seamless data access and flow across the institution. This will contribute to promoting cross-department collaboration, replication, and upscaling of good practices; a better understanding of the status and trends as well as the threats and drivers behind biodiversity loss, environmental degradation, escalating pollution; and the interdependencies between environmental sustainability, climate and disaster risk reduction, and sector operations. ADB will facilitate access to research, case studies, best practices, and comprehensive data on environmental impact, policy, finance, and projects at regional and subregional, national, and subnational levels.

ADB will enhance its knowledge-sharing mechanisms to promote nature-positive and mainstream actions in DMCs, including in both the public and private sectors. ADB will be hosting workshops, seminars, and training, in addition to convening regional and subregional forums and flagship events such as the Asia Clean Energy Forum, Better Air Quality, and Healthy Oceans Forum to support policymakers and key stakeholders to exchange insights and build partnerships. ADB will foster ongoing engagement among experts to advance knowledge on co-benefits across different sectors' investments and practices. Strategic partnerships with academic institutions, international organizations, and development banks will amplify these efforts.

ADB will continue to prepare knowledge products in the form of publications, articles, audiovisual material, digital resources, and other innovative ways to showcase experiences on design and implementation of nature-positive and mainstreaming projects; and provide thought leadership and up-to-date information on biodiversity, pollution, and climate change. This will be prepared with a view to enable replication and scaling up of such measures and inform the design of future nature-positive investments and environmentally sustainable projects.

Supporting capacity development and training. ADB will continue to provide training workshops, webinars, and capacity development programs on critical environmental topics targeted at key stakeholders who often play a major role in designing, implementing, and monitoring projects. ADB will build the capacity of DMCs to meaningfully engage young people in environmental and climate action at the regional, national, and local levels, for inclusive and innovative investments. Similarly, ADB will utilize its subregional frameworks to build capacity to coordinate regional responses to address transboundary assets, formulate focused solutions for specific regional challenges, and standardize environmental management practices to uniformly manage shared resources. Training content will also include the application of new technologies, best practices, analyses of investment constraints and opportunities, and innovative financing mechanisms for the environment.

Furthermore, detailed strategies for capacity development at the national and regional levels will be implemented, ensuring countries and regions possess the skills and technology necessary to manage their environment and biodiversity data systems effectively. This involves training, workshops, and technical resources to enhance the skills of personnel involved in biodiversity monitoring and data management. ADB will support the development of national and regional biodiversity and ecosystem information systems, and real-time inventory pollution monitoring, and build capacity to further the adoption of mapping tools to minimize the impact of sovereign and nonsovereign operations on the environment in DMCs.

In addition, trainings will also be organized to develop the guidelines for and facilitate the implementation of environment, social, and governance considerations into financial management assessments; the adoption of sustainability financial reporting standards; and the auditing of nature-related expenditures. Finally, ADB will prepare tiered knowledge solutions around the three pillars that systematically build technical capacity not only of external clients but also internal personnel to design, implement, monitor, and adaptively manage environment-related projects; and further develop cooperation with knowledge partners including CSOs, academia, Indigenous Peoples, and local communities. These include knowledge interventions on the EAP itself for effective and efficient implementation.

Adopting digital technologies and artificial intelligence. ADB will take advantage of the rapid growth of digital technologies and tools including artificial intelligence and the Internet of Things to develop and implement effective nature-positive and mainstreaming projects. The use of digital tools and platforms will be promoted to enable efficient and accurate data collection and analysis to influence decision making on the location and design of nature-based solutions and nature-positive and mainstreaming projects. For example, use of the Avian Sensitivity Tool for Energy Planning tool will be encouraged to inform the location of wind and solar farms, including transmission lines to avoid key biodiversity areas and flyways and at the same time maximize tapping of solar and wind energy.

Remote sensing, geographic information system, and other landscape and seascape level planning tools will be promoted for conducting strategic environmental assessments to inform the location and design of infrastructure and nature-based solutions. In addition, such tools together with sensor systems and artificial intelligence will be promoted for comprehensive ecosystem monitoring, transparent carbon trading, and real-time pollution tracking in projects. Internet of Things-based environment monitoring will support and drastically increase efficiency in gathering and analyzing environment-related data, such as air and water quality, soil properties, and ecosystems, for informed decision making and improved project design and adaptive management. Digital platforms will be used to promote inclusive community engagement in conservation efforts, improving policy effectiveness and environmental stewardship. Digital platforms and networks will be developed and strengthened to promote the exchange of data, best practices, innovative solutions, and lessons learned to address environmental challenges. Digital tools can also facilitate ongoing dialogue and collect continuous feedback, ensuring that stakeholder voices are heard and integrated into project planning and execution phases of environment projects. Finally, digital technologies and artificial intelligence could potentially help reduce monitoring and reporting costs over time.

IV INTEGRATED APPROACH TOWARD SYNERGY

ADB will adopt a holistic approach to place environment and nature as its core focus and a key part of its climate change and private sector shifts. This strategic shift will not only help reverse nature loss but also promote sustainable growth opportunities, greener jobs, and improved water and food security, while adjusting longstanding development processes to better adapt and align against changing environment.

Environment and nature are invariably interconnected with climate change mitigation and adaptation, and disaster risk management. Nature provides viable solutions for climate mitigation and adaptation, notably through carbon storage and restoration of degraded ecosystems. Furthermore, nature-positive investments are likely to provide additional disaster risk management benefits if such investments are guided by (i) disaster risk information, (ii) clearly articulated disaster risk reduction objectives, (iii) hazard-specific mitigation expertise, and (iv) community engagement. Therefore, EAP, CCAP, and DRMAP will collaborate—starting with a focus on selected areas and countries—to enhance (i) integrated planning and implementation, (ii) complementary financing and investments, (iii) coordinated capacity development initiatives, (iv) effective knowledge management and communication efforts, and (v) synergistic monitoring and reporting frameworks. This strategic alignment aims to optimize resource use, maximize co-benefits, and achieve targeted outcomes more effectively.

Environment and nature are integral components for all of ADB's sector work. The bank will leverage the sector synergies and further develop guidance notes and references to promote nature-positive investments and mainstreaming environment in sector investments. These efforts will not only benefit the environment but also enhance the efficiency and sustainability of sector projects, creating mutual benefits across all areas of engagement. ADB recognizes that urban and rural settings have significantly different needs for natural resources management due to differences in land use and infrastructure, population density, resource consumption and waste, economic activities, and environmental impact. ADB will address these distinctions in devising effective and efficient solutions to tackle environmental issues in the specific contexts.

Beyond Sector Groups, themes that are of relevance to environment and nature include gender, regional cooperation and integration, and fragile and conflict-affected situations and small island developing states contexts. ADB will ensure that gender considerations are included in all aspects of environment and nature initiatives. ADB recognizes that environmental degradation, loss of biodiversity and nature, and rampant pollution can be significant threat multipliers for fragile and conflict-affected situations and small island developing states. Therefore, it will ensure that the specific needs of these countries are addressed by both ensuring a deep understanding of circumstances and exploring tailored economic, environmental, and social interventions to deliver relevant assistance in complex operational contexts. Priorities will include strengthening institutional frameworks, promoting community-based approaches for sustainable natural resource management, leveraging nature-based solutions to build and enhance climate and disaster resilience, integrating environmental sustainability into conflict resolution efforts, developing necessary capacity, and implementing robust pollution control measures to prevent worsening of complexities.

Nature-positive investments will be designed to enhance progress and identify new opportunities to enhance women's empowerment and gender equality in societies and economies while strengthening women's resilience to external shocks. The important role of women in biodiversity and ecosystem management, particularly among Indigenous Peoples and local communities is well recognized, especially in improving project outcomes. Positive results will also be pursued by enhancing women's participation and addressing inequalities in accessing resources. Gender inclusivity will also be built into capacity building efforts, empowering all community members to participate in the design, implementation, and monitoring of nature-based solutions and nature-positive investments. ADB will also explore novel financing models that reward women's groups for ecosystem stewardship, such as protecting forests and adopting environmentally sustainable agriculture practices. Finally, gender-responsive environmental assessments and diagnostics will be implemented to ensure relevant strategy and project development with concrete activities, budgets, and results that promote gender equality and women's empowerment. This will be applied by drawing out experiences and lessons through ongoing gender initiatives such as the TA on Strengthening Women's Resilience to Heat Stress in Asia and the Pacific.

V IMPLEMENTATION ARRANGEMENTS

All departments across ADB are responsible and will work together toward successful EAP implementation. Responsibilities will be allocated along the lines of business processes such as integrating environment and nature into country partnership strategy and country pipelines and integrating environmental sustainability into the design of grants, loans, and other operational tasks. CCSD will facilitate coherence in the implementation of this action plan, provide technical guidance and coordination, help capture lessons and knowledge solutions, provide thought leadership on increasing and emerging challenges and opportunities, and test new approaches and innovations through pilot projects.

Each department will identify and utilize appropriate entry points within business processes to initiate and sustain positive environmental actions. For example, CCSD and Agriculture, Food, Nature, and Rural Development Sector Office are co-leading to prepare an approach paper on natural capital to streamline and scale up natural capital investments, including use of natural capital assessment and accounting to promote sustainable agriculture and food systems.

To strengthen internal coordination, the Environment Community of Practice (CoP) was established to foster collaboration, knowledge sharing, and the development of best practices for projects between ADB Staff and consultants with a shared interest in environmental issues and sustainability. Membership is voluntary and members are welcome to participate in one or more of the CoP working groups on (i) biodiversity and ecosystem management, (ii) air quality, (iii) circular economy, (iv) environment and climate finance, and (v) nature-based solutions. Its activities and initiatives align with ADB's Strategy 2030 goals and policies related to environmental sustainability. The Environment CoP's terms of reference will be periodically reviewed and updated to ensure that it continually meets its objectives and remains in step with ADB's goals. Its effectiveness will also be regularly evaluated for its impact on ADB's environmental sustainability efforts and identify areas for improvement. The COP and its five issue-based working groups will promote thought leadership necessary to mainstream environmental sustainability in ADB's operations. They will develop platforms for effective knowledge sharing and leverage cross-sector expertise and opportunities to enhance the bank's capability to address environmental challenges proactively and innovatively.

Climate Change and Sustainable Development Department (CCSD). CCSD will provide thought leadership and be responsible for the overall coordination, facilitation, and tracking of the EAP implementation. It also plays a key role in promoting regional cooperation, forming strategic partnerships, delivering targeted assistance, pursuing equality and inclusion, and mobilizing resources effectively to address biodiversity loss, pollutions, and climate change. CCSD will also ensure that the action plan activities are gender-inclusive and engage CSOs, local communities, and Indigenous Peoples. Additionally, the CCSD is responsible for the communication and dissemination of the EAP and will establish mechanisms for scheduled reviews and feedback incorporation to refine and improve the plan. CCSD will work closely with all departments for successful EAP implementation.

Sector Groups. Sector groups will play a critical role in leading the processing and implementation of nature-positive investment, nature-based solutions, and environmental sustainability projects. Key environment flagship programs of ADB such as the Healthy Ocean Action Plan, Regional Flyway Initiative, and Asia Clean Blue Skies Program include investment projects under the agriculture, food, nature, and rural development; energy; public financial management; and other sectors that are being led by the Sector Groups. Sectors involving infrastructure development such as transport, energy, urban, agriculture and others will consider integrating nature-based solutions and mainstreaming environmental sustainability in project design as relevant. In addition, Sector Groups will be utilizing the updated project classification system that would allow for better project tagging and monitoring, including their environment-related aspects and other updated business processes for preparing and implementing projects.

Regional departments and resident missions. They will play a critical role in promoting nature-positive investments and mainstreaming environment at the upstream level. Resident missions will engage directly with DMCs and lead the preparation of country partnership strategies (CPS) and advance the development of a pipeline of nature-positive investments based on guidance and active support from CCSD, Sectors Group, Office of Markets Development and Public–Private Partnership, and Private Sector Operations Department. This will include conducting national diagnostic studies on the state of environment and natural resources management in relation to climate change and disaster risk management to inform the CPS on priority nature-positive and environmentally sustainable investments. Similarly, in collaboration with CCSD, regional departments can leverage their respective regional cooperation frameworks (i.e., GMS, CAREC, and SASEC) to formulate long-term strategies and regional work plans to promote nature-positive investments from a subregional perspective. Regional departments will address environmental public goods by coordinating collaborative natural resource management, encouraging the standardization of legislation, promoting data and research sharing, harmonizing development plans, establishing regional funding mechanisms, and increasing awareness on regional public goods.

Private Sector Operations Department (PSOD) and Office of Markets Development and Public–Private Partnership (OMDP). The private sector is recognized as a key stakeholder for financing and scaling up nature-positive investments, nature-based solutions, and environmental sustainability in projects. Hence, PSOD will collaborate with CCSD and the Sector Groups to engage with the private sector on projects including sustainable agricultural production, natural resources supply chain management, waste management, and greening of industries. OMDP, in collaboration with CCSD and the Sector Groups, will provide advisory services to DMCs in designing and implementing public–private partnership (PPP) initiatives, and developing carbon markets, market development, and innovative financing to promote nature-based investments and conservation. While PSOD's client is the private sector, OMDP's main client is the government, supporting policy development and providing institutional capacity building for its PPP units. This includes PPP 101 training delivered through ADB's Public–Private Partnership Academy, featuring PPP's role in sustainable infrastructure development among its topics.

Non-operational corporate departments. ADB's departments that are not directly engaged in operational projects (i.e., non-operational departments) will continue to reduce institutional barriers and create an enabling corporate environment for mainstreaming environmental sustainability into ADB operations and portfolio. This includes but is not limited to the following:

(i) **Strategic management.** Key to successful EAP implementation are the efforts of the Strategy, Policy, and Partnerships Department (SPD) to harmonize the corporate results framework indicators with other MDBs around biodiversity and nature-positive investments. SPD's guidance will also be key for exploring CCSD's proposed updates to the project classification system and sovereign operations system for effective and efficient environment-related program and project monitoring, evaluation, and reporting at the corporate level. Moreover, SPD's work on designing a financial incentives framework to drive and support nature-positive investments from ADB's DMCs is synergistically aligned with EAP's downstream engagement. The Economic Research and Development Impact Department's work on developing guidelines and database tools for the valuation of ecosystem services (Box 10), upstreaming support on ADB project economic analysis, piloting research on natural capital accounting, and developing the environmentally extended multiregional input–output tables are critical in ensuring that the value of nature is not only recognized but also effectively incorporated into investment planning, project design, and relevant policies in the region. This helps align ADB with the global direction increasingly linking economic health and financial stability with healthy environments.

(ii) **Finance and risk management.** The controller's engagement in the Task Force on Nature-related Financial Disclosures framework, or a similar standard under the International Sustainability Standards Board, prepares ADB to participate in global discussions on assessing and disclosing its relationship with nature for better informed, environmentally sustainable financial decision-making. As ADB explores innovative and more complex lending opportunities, the Office of Risk Management can contribute directly to risk identification assessment, reporting, and mitigation, allowing ADB to expand its role as Asia's climate bank. Meanwhile, the Treasury Department continues to explore various themes across markets and currencies as well as evaluate outcome-related bond issuances.

(iii) **Corporate administration.** Together with CCSD and SPD, Information Technology Department; Budget, Personnel, and Management Systems Department (BPMSD); and Procurement, Portfolio, and Financial Management Department will be important collaborators in building the technical capacity of ADB and its projects, filling the skills gaps needed for successful EAP implementation through a Build–Buy–Borrow–Bots approach. BPMSD will help operational teams "build" in-house skills through reskilling, re-balancing the skills mix and/or recruiting new skills. PPFD will help "buy" the skills through consultancy services. CCSD and SPD will facilitate to "borrow" the skills through partnerships, while the Information Technology Department, with CCSD, will deliver "bots" by leveraging technology such as automation and artificial intelligence to deliver work. In collaboration with the Procurement, Portfolio and Financial Management Department and Corporate Services Department initiatives on increasing ADB and DMCs' capacity for sustainable procurement (Box 13), EAP will further collaborate with these departments on building a network of suppliers to support nature-positive and ecologically friendly design components integration in project design and implementation. As the Office of the Secretary continues to deliver an increasingly sustainable ADB Annual Meeting, organizing this event also provides an opportunity for building an in-country network of partners, suppliers, and service providers that can support an environmentally sustainable agenda on the ground. CSD's work on making ADB's facilities and services more environmentally sustainable also demonstrates ADB's leadership in practicing what it preaches (Box 18).

Box 18: Green ADB

The Institutional Climate Secretariat, chaired by Corporate Services Department, is developing long-term carbon reduction and environmentally sustainable options. This will allow ADB to establish a road map to reduce its carbon footprint generated from its institutional operations, such as facilities, procurement, transportation and business travel, and waste management. ADB continues to adopt more environmentally sustainable habits and practices, including initiatives and partnerships to "green" its facilities, literally and figuratively, through the introduction of solar panels, electric vehicle charging infrastructure, and requiring new field offices to occupy facilities with sustainability certification, such as LEED, EDGE, WELL or other similar certification. The Institutional Climate Secretariat is also advocating to turn the headquarters and field offices into environmental flagships, demonstrating ADB's commitment to a greener planet. These initiatives could include covering buildings with plants and foliage, introducing atmospheric water generation, adopting new battery storage technology for cleaner power as opposed to diesel generators, and removing the gas station from the ADB compound while adding facilities for electric vehicles and pedal bikes.

Source: Asian Development Bank.

(iv) **Office of Safeguards.** This office is coordinating comprehensive review and update of ADB's Safeguard Policy Statement. The upcoming environmental and social framework will play an important role in the operationalization of the EAP, especially with the potential adoption of a performance standards model[35] with a stand-alone policy statement on environmental and social sustainability; and several separate performance standards which will set out the requirements that apply to ADB projects. Specifically, the proposed environmental and social framework will include (a) ADB's vision on environmental and social sustainability; (b) an environmental and social stability policy which sets out mandatory responsibilities to ADB; (c) the 10 Environmental and Social Standards and include a standard on biodiversity conservation and sustainable natural resources management, resource conservation and pollution prevention and climate change; (d) requirements for financing modalities and products; and (e) the Prohibited Investment Activity List, defined with nature, ecosystems, biodiversity, pollution prevention, and resource use efficiency. Moreover, the office's integrated safeguard management system (ISMS) will play a key role for ADB to capture project impacts on biodiversity, helping it gain a portfolio-wide view on biodiversity, both positive and negative.

(v) **Other non-operational corporate departments.** The General Counsel is critical in helping strengthen legal and regulatory frameworks, as well as effectively implementing and enforcing laws that support nature and environment sustainability in ADB's DMCs (Box 19). The Department of Communications and Knowledge Management is critical to the EAP in positively transforming the sociopolitical and institutional environments and increasing their absorptive capacity for environmental sustainability interventions; through development communications (e.g., information dissemination and education, social marketing, social mobilization, media advocacy, and socialization of environmental sustainability technologies and approaches); as well as the organization of knowledge creation across the tacit and explicit knowledge dimensions.

---

[35] A performance standard model is followed by EBRD, IDB, IFC, and WB and has a modular approach. The structure includes (i) a stand-alone institutional commitment/policy statement on environmental and social sustainability; and (ii) 8–10 separate standards that cover which set-out requirements that apply to borrowers. These standards define client responsibilities and provide direction for managing environmental and social risks in projects.

Box 19: Law and Policy Reform Program

The Law and Policy Reform (LPR) Program led by the Office of the General Counsel is helping to strengthen legal and regulatory frameworks and implementation and enforcement of laws to support investments in nature and environmental sustainability in ADB developing member countries (DMCs). For example, the LPR Program is supporting the Model Forest Act Initiative to develop a comprehensive and innovative legal blueprint for legislators, policymakers, and other stakeholders in designing a modern legal framework for the protection, conservation, restoration, and ecologically sustainable management and use of forests. Furthermore, the LPR Program is working with legal and judicial stakeholders such as environmental legal educators and institutions and judiciaries to improve implementation and enforcement of environmental protection laws. At the same time, the LPR Program is supporting DMCs to establish or modernize laws fundamental to attracting private finance to increase nature-positive investments. Updated information is available online at the Environment and Climate Change pages of ADB's Law and Policy Reform Program website.

Source: ADB's Law and Policy Reform Program.

VI MONITORING AND REPORTING ARRANGEMENTS

The List of Environment Actions (Appendix 1) will be reviewed and updated annually under the leadership of the environment group of the CCSD, reviewed by an ad hoc EAP working group consisting of representatives from relevant teams and approved by the CCSD director-general. A midterm review of the EAP will be conducted in 2027 to enable adaptive management of its implementation.

A robust monitoring and results framework will be developed to monitor the progress of the EAP. The development impact, outcome, and indicators under the framework will be aligned with the revised corporate results framework. The outputs will reflect the upstream, midstream, downstream, and crosscutting measures for operationalization of the EAP as provided in section III and the proposed actions in Appendix 1. Tracking of nature positive financing and mainstreaming of environment sustainability in sector operations will be conducted through an updated project classification system and an appropriate tracking system, which is being explored. Tracking of nature-positive finance will be aligned with the approach currently under development and to be agreed between the MDBs under the *Joint Statement on Nature, Peoples and Planet*. The revised project classification system will allow aggregation and disaggregation of data to show portfolio-wide numbers that can be used for future disclosure requirements, issuing of thematic bonds, including in Development Effectiveness Review and other relevant reports.

Annual progress reports on EAP implementation will be prepared and shared with the Board for information. The report will include information on overall progress made against the monitoring and results framework, and key accomplishments including progress on the key environment action items provided in Appendix 1. It will also include an outlook for the coming year with key opportunities and any adaptive action that needs to be taken. Components of the EAP contributing to climate change mitigation and adaptation and disaster risk management will be highlighted and contributions to climate finance calculated as per ADB's guidance. Contribution to other important cross-cutting themes such as gender-related results, stakeholder engagement, regional cooperation and integration, and digital technology will also be reflected. A midterm review of the EAP will be conducted in 2027 and shared with the Board and stakeholders for information, to take stock of its progress and make needed updates to enable adaptive management in its implementation. A final report on the EAP implementation will be initiated by the environment group at the end of 2030 to assess its results and draw lessons for a future strategic approach.

LIST OF ENVIRONMENT ACTIONS

The table below outlines the initial planned actions that ADB will take vis-a-vis enhancing environmental sustainability across its operations and beyond under the environment action plan. It specifies responsible departments and groups accountable for executing each action and the estimated timeline.

	Action	Target Date	Responsibility
A	**Upstream Engagement**		
A1	**Mainstream Nature Positive Investments and Environmental Sustainability in Country Partnership Strategies (CPS).**		
	1. Conduct integrated, gender-responsive diagnostic studies on environment, including valuation of natural capital, biodiversity, and pollution, in coordination with climate change and disaster risk management and safeguards, to inform the inclusion of nature-positive and environmentally sustainable programs in the CPS in at least 12 DMCs.	Dec 2027	RMs as lead with support from CCRE-ENV, Sectors Group, OMDP, PSOD, OSFG
	2. Prepare internal guidance to promote mainstreaming of nature positive investments and environmental sustainability in CPS.	Dec 2025	CCRE-ENV
	3. Participate in annual country programming and indicative country pipeline and monitoring (ICMP) reporting.	2024–2030	CCRE-ENV
A2	**Improve ADB's corporate systems for monitoring and reporting on environment and nature projects.**		
	1. Update environmental sustainability outcome indicator as part of the updating exercise of ADB's corporate results framework and establish key metrics and monitoring system for environment and nature projects. These metrics will also support reporting against future standards such as Taskforce on Nature-related Financial Disclosures (TNFD).	Dec 2024	SPD, OSFG
	2. In close coordination with SPD, explore ways to improve the project classification system (PCS) and sovereign operations (SOVOPs) systems to ensure more accurate accounting of sector and subsector project with environment and nature activities and components.	Dec 2026	CCRE-ENV

continued on next page

Table continued

		Action	Target Date	Responsibility
A		**Upstream Engagement**		
		3. Draft internal guidance for tagging environment and nature investments in sector projects in close coordination with SPD. This will also include guidance on entry points and approaches for promoting environment and nature activities and components in sector investments.	Dec 2025	CCRE-ENV
		4. Explore designing a financial incentives framework to incentivize and support nature- positive investments while promoting equality and inclusion from ADB's DMCs.	2025	SPD
		5. Map out and build on existing operational systems and processes to support effective implementation of the EAP with a view to reduce additional burden/processes for staff.	2025	CCRE-ENV
		6. Contribute to the preparation of ADB's Sustainability Report.	2026	CCRE-ENV, CTL
B		**Midstream Engagement**		
B1		**Supporting related policies and regulations.**		
		1. Support at least 5 DMCs in improving environment and biodiversity conservation- related laws, policies, or regulations including strengthening institutional capacity and coordination in coordination with the Law and Policy Reform Program (LPR) being led by OGC.	Dec 2027	CCRE-ENV, OGC, OSFG
		2. Support DMCs' efforts in addressing CSOs, Indigenous Peoples and local communities, and gender inclusion in environment and nature initiatives through CPS and relevant activities and identify opportunities for capacity development and knowledge exchange.	2027	CCGE, CCFE
B2		**Programming and technical support.**		
		1. Conduct diagnostic studies targeted at key landscapes, seascapes, and airsheds in coordination with safeguards to develop pipeline of investment projects with sector groups for addressing biodiversity loss and pollution through regional initiatives, including but not limited to the following: a. Regional Flyway Initiative b. Circular economy and plastic pollution c. Building Coastal Resilience through Nature–Based and Integrated Solutions d. Asia Clean Blue Skies Program	Dec 2027	CCRE-ENV, OSFG

continued on next page

Table continued

	Action	Target Date	Responsibility
B	**Midstream Engagement**		
	2. Promote Nature-Based Solutions in PPP projects.	2027	OMDP
	3. Integrate landscape level environmental assessments into sector-based master planning exercises.	2027	CCRE-ENV, OSFG, SGs
	4. Pilot natural capital assessment and accounting in 5 DMCs (ongoing: Armenia, PRC, Cook Islands, Philippines, and Sri Lanka)	2025	AFNR, ERDI, CCSD
	5. Integrate environmental priorities into DMC public finance management.	2027	SG-PSMG, RM
	6. Integrate environmental priorities into DMC public procurement systems.	2026	PPFD, RM
	7. Develop and implement guidelines for including environmental, social, and governance (ESG) considerations in financial management assessments.		PPFD
B3	**Promoting innovative finance.**		
	1. Manage the Nature Solutions Finance Hub and continue to catalyze more funds through the hub for creating a pipeline of environment and nature projects. This includes developing guides and training courses including on NBS and environmental considerations in PPP initiatives; and design projects with financial structure that increases revenue streams	2027	CCRE-ENV and SG-FIN
	2. Develop new and innovative finance instruments to support nature investments like biodiversity and nature bonds, debt-for-nature swaps, and outcome-based bonds.	Dec 2027	TD, SG-FIN, and CCRE-ENV
	3. Review harmful subsidies to environment and explore ways to shift finance for environment and nature investment.	2027	SG-FIN, CCRE-ENV
B4	**Promoting Environmentally Sustainable Procurement.**		
	1. Develop guidance and related training materials on environmentally sound approaches and nature-based solution criteria and specifications for ADB infrastructure project procurement. Update the Sustainable Procurement Resource Hub with guidance on nature-based solutions relevant to development operations.	Dec 2025	PPFD, CCRE-ENV
	2. Undertake market research and engagement to support the development of sustainable supply chain for five DMCs, focusing on heavy construction materials	June 2025	PPFD, RDs, PSOD

continued on next page

Table continued

	Action	Target Date	Responsibility
B	**Midstream Engagement**		
B5	**Cross-Sector Integration and Regional Cooperation.**		
	1. Foster regional cooperation to address transboundary environment issues, including air quality and integrated wetland, water, and coastal management initiatives, in the Mekong subregion and the Indo-Gangetic Plains and Hindu Kush Himalaya, including design and implementation of TA and investment projects.	Dec 2027	CCRE-ENV
	2. Foster regional cooperation to address plastic pollution through support for regional (or subregional) dialogues, formation of regional working groups, creation of regional laws, regional declarations, or framework for action in line with the Global Plastic Treaty.	Dec 2027	CCRE-ENV
	3. Provide internal guidance to support identification and design of investments in regional public goods for environmental management.	2025	CCRE-ENV
C	**Downstream Engagement**		
C1	**Scale up nature positive investments on:**		
	1. Wetland restoration, river basin management, and river revitalization	2024–2027	RMs, RDs, SG-AFNR, SG-WUD, OMDP, PSOD
	2. Green value chain and infrastructure development projects		
	3. Water supply and sanitation		
	4. Air quality improvement		
	5. Solid waste management including plastic pollution		
	6. PPP carbon credits for ecosystems including forests, grasslands, peatlands and mangroves		
	7. Biodiversity conservation and ecotourism		
C2	**Mainstream environmental sustainability into sector investments with biodiversity and ecosystem management, pollution reduction or nature-based solution as a key co-benefit through the following measures:**		
	1. Promote renewable energy, energy efficiency, and clean heating and cooling in energy sector projects	2024–2027	SG–AFNR, SG–WUD, SG–ENE, SG–TRA, RMs, RDs, OSFG, OMDP, PSOD

continued on next page

Table continued

	Action	Target Date	Responsibility
C	**Downstream Engagement**		
	2. Enhance climate and disaster resilience and biodiversity conservation through nature-based solutions in projects on coastal cities 3. Promote nature-based solutions in projects involving riverbank protection and flood risk management 4. Integrate biodiversity friendly measures in transport infrastructure 5. Strengthen climate resilience through mangrove rehabilitation in the Mekong Delta 6. Promote investments on sustainable coastal and fisheries management 7. Improve solid waste management		
D	**Crosscutting Measures**		
D1	**Strengthen partnerships and stakeholder engagement.**		
	1. Lead or actively contribute to collaborative efforts for promoting nature positive and mainstreaming projects and programs.	Dec 2025	CCRE-ENV, SPD
	2. Strengthen existing and new partnerships, including Agence Française de Developpement (AFD), Birdlife International, East Asian-Australasian Flyway Partnership (EAAFP), GCF, GEF, Japan Ministry of Environment, The Nature Conservancy, World Wide Fund for Nature (WWF), CGIAR, World Resources Institute, leading universities, and other MDBs for leveraging technical and/or financial resources for addressing environmental challenges and enabling broader impacts.	Dec 2027	CCRE-ENV
D2	**Knowledge Generation and Sharing.**		
	1. Organize events that are science-based, showcase innovative tools and approaches, and focus on operationalizing and scaling up nature positive and mainstreaming activities and components in sectors and private sector projects and programs.	2025	CCRE-ENV
	2. Prepare approach paper on natural capital, including ecosystem valuation tools for project economic analysis.	2025	SG-AFNR, ERDI, CCRE-ENV
	3. Prepare natural capital assessment and ecosystem valuation tools for project economic analysis.	2025	ERDI
	4. Prepare a publication on natural capitals to share experiences in Asia and the Pacific.	2027	ERDI

continued on next page

Table continued

	Action	Target Date	Responsibility
D	**Crosscutting Measures**		
D2	5. Prepare a knowledge product and webinar on gender responsive nature-based cooling solutions, in connection with the ADB Task Force on Gender and Heat Stress.	2024	CCRE-ENV
	6. Organize a webinar series on Green Road to Cali in the lead up to the CBD COP in Oct/Nov 2024.	2024	CCRE-ENV
	7. Lead ADB's participation in key global and regional events on environment and nature that are closely linked with ADB's operations such as CBD COP, Convention on Migratory Species (CMS) COP, Climate Change COP, Ramsar Convention COP, Better Air Quality conference and others.	Dec 2027	CCRE-ENV
	8. Organize event on the Regional Flyway Initiative at the East Asian-Australasian Flyway Partnership 12th Meeting of Parties (MOP12) in the Philippines and other opportunities.	Nov 2025	CCRE-ENV, PHCO
	9. Strengthening communication on environment and nature: Develop key communications outputs to support the environment action plan (EAP). The proposed EAP communications will be in synergy with the communications supporting the climate change action plan and the (proposed) disaster risk management action plan.	Dec 2025	DOCK
	10. Prepare a publication on engaging youth in nature positive investments for greater inclusivity and impact.	Sep 2027	CCRE-ENV
D3	**Training and Capacity Building.**		
	1. Organize a training session on nature-positive investments and natural capital approaches with a focus on climate–food–nature nexus in collaboration with ADBI and AFNR.	Dec 2027	CCRE-ENV, AFNR, OSFG, CCGE, BPCT
	2. Organize trainings workshops in collaboration with safeguards on air quality, circular economy and others targeted for DMCs, ADB Staff, CSOs, consultants, and others.	2027	PPFD
	3. Organize training workshops on marine biodiversity and coastal resilience, wetland conservation, and nature-based solutions in investment projects, and others targeted at DMCs, local communities, and ADB Staff.	Nov 2025	OGC
	4. Organize training workshops on Green PFM, ESG considerations, implementation of sustainability financial reporting standards, and auditing environment related expenditures for DMCs and ADB Staff.	Dec 2027	CCRE-ENV, BPCT

continued on next page

Table continued

	Action	Target Date	Responsibility
D	**Crosscutting Measures**		
D3	5. Knowledge sharing on the Model Forest Act under the Model Forest Act Initiative supported under OGC's Legal Toolkit for the Protection of Vital Ecosystems for Climate, Biodiversity, and Livelihoods. 6. Compile, expand and promote existing online learning resources on environment and nature.		
D4	**Adopting digital technologies and artificial intelligence (AI)** 1. Promote use of digital tools and technology for advancing nature positive and environmentally sustainable investments such as remote sensing, GIS, AI, IoT and others for landscape level planning, strategic environmental assessments, ecosystem monitoring, carbon trading, pollution tracking, stakeholder engagement, preventing human–wildlife conflicts etc.	Dec 2027	CCRE-ENV; CCDT
	2. Collaborate on training programs on digital technology on topics related to environment and nature for various stakeholders.	Dec 2027	CCRE-ENV; CCDT, ITD

AFNR = Agriculture, Food, Nature, and Rural Development Sector Office; BPCT = Culture and Talent Division; CCDT = Digital Technology for Development Division; CCFE = Fragility and Engagement Division; CCGE = Gender Equality Division; CTL = Controller's Department; CCRE-ENV = Climate Change, Resilience, and Environment Cluster – Environment; DOCK = Department of Communications and Knowledge Management; ERDI = Economic Research and Development Impact Department; ITD = Information Technology Department; OGC = Office of the General Counsel; OMDP = Office of Markets Development and Public–Private Partnership; OSFG = Office of Safeguards; PHCO = Philippine Country Office; PPFD = Procurement, Portfolio, and Financial Management Department; PSOD = Private Sector Operations Department; RD = regional department; RM = resident mission; SG = Sector Group; SG–FIN = Finance Sector Office; SG–PSMG Public Sector Management and Governance Sector Office; SG–WUD = Water and Urban Development Sector Office; SPD = Strategy, Policy, and Partnerships Department; TD = Treasury Department.

SWOT ANALYSIS ON ENVIRONMENT ACTIONS IN ADB OPERATIONS

STRENGTHS

- ADB operations span across multiple sectors and ES is embedded in varied levels across sectors.
- Access to substantial and diverse financial resources and instruments.
- Extensive network and partnerships that amplify impact and reach.
- Over 5 decades of extensive expertise and experience and alignment with global commitments.
- Well positioned to influence environmental policy in DMCs.
- Strong regional perspective and focus on regional cooperation.

WEAKNESSES

- Primarily perceived as operational safeguard rather than strategic function, restricts advancement of environmental agenda.
- Inconsistent policies and capacity contraints limit environmental impact.
- Fragmented implementation, weak linkages between initiatives, complexity in strategic focus, and lack of prioritization.
- Limited fiscal space, insufficient concessional funding, and inadequate governance in DMCs, variability in execution effectiveness across sectors.
- Complex bureaucracy and institutional structures complicate coordination across departments.
- Insufficient monitoring and tracking systems, underused innovations and technologies.

SWOT

OPPORTUNITIES

- Global alignments, expanding partnerships, and leveraging growing environmental interests and awareness.
- Utilize ADB's reputation to scale up environmental agenda.
- Utilize innovative financing models and engage private sector investment.
- Advanced and emerging technologies to address and improve environmental management.
- Integrate environmental considerations into economic analyses and project funding decisions.
- Build on synergies between climate and nature and boost transboundary cooperation to address transboundary issues, expanding influence in underrepresented areas.

THREATS

- Competing agendas and priorities could create resource conflicts.
- Political instability and economic pressures may lead to deprioritization of envrionmental agenda.
- Unpredictability and intensification of climate impacts can exacerbate environmental degredation.
- Challenges in balancing economic growth with sustainability.
- Variability in regulations across DMCs impedes consistent and standardized implementation.
- Ensuring broad public support and engagement is critical.